Pol

Polyamorou

Understanding Polyamourous Relationships; A Helpful and Practical Guide.

By

Wenyan Lee

Table of Contents

Introduction

Polyamory requires the ability to make plans, and follow through reliably. It requires immense amounts of communication, which is heard and acknowledged so that misunderstandings are few. It requires everyone involved to respect each other as a human, with inalienable rights to time and focused attention with their lovers. It requires folks to realize they are all equal, and not behave competitively. It requires folks to realize they will get more time with some lovers, and less time with others, because there are only so many hours available. Polyamory requires lovers to realize their lovers will make mistakes, and chose poor partners sometimes, and will require space to figure out how to choose partners that are healthy and beneficial to their lives. We are all fallible.

Polyamory requires us to be self-aware enough to examine our own lives, and learn to deal with our issues, to come to peace with our past, instead of taking out our problems on others. It requires us always to be the better person and love people through their drama, without trying to fix them. It requires us to learn from our lessons, and allow others to learn theirs, as slowly and repeatedly as necessary.

Monogamous people get married and expect that person to love them and only them forever. Humans don't love just one person, ever. Even in monogamous relationships, people love other people in their lives: friends, family, co-workers and their children. They draw strength from friends that love and support them. They have intimate conversations with other humans that can lead to sexual feelings. Often, monogamous people will cheat at this point. But polyamorous people don't have to cheat. They get to love anyone and everyone to the degree that suits them. There is no end to how many you can love, and how you love them. The only limit is how much time you have for everyone in your life. This happens with friendships too. I have many intimate friendships with people I adore and want in my life forever, but I don't need to live with them to love them. Some I will probably live with eventually, some I just

4

like to hang with occasionally, and some I need to talk to regularly, to help me see my path.

Polyamory is not an evolution of relationships, and it's going back to relationship origins when tribal members cared for each other. There will be folk in the tribe who create chaos and need to be dealt with, often by loving them more, but sometimes by leaving them behind to think and grow. There will be some relationships that are more intense than others. There will be some that are more free and casual, less attached than others, but love is not quantifiable. All love is the same love, and valuable for the warm feelings alone, regardless of where those feelings lead.

Polyamory

Polyamory is the ability to carry on more than one relationship at a time. When a loved one needs you, you can be there for them, emotionally and physically, usually with a large support group to draw upon. Polyamory is the ability to prioritize your time, so everyone with whom you are in love gets the attention they need to feel important.

Polyamory is saying you will be responsible and fulfill the commitments you make just as you would with any romantic relationship. Polyamory is loving and caring for many people, and many people are loving and caring for you.

Monogamy

Monogamy is a loving commitment to love and usually having sex with only one person.

One issue, which often comes up, is that a polyamorous person falls in love with a monogamous person. Since a monogamous person is one who can only commit to one person at a time, they only have the focus, time and attention for that person, and they want to be that one special person in their lover's life. They are seeking a dynamic that is loyal and fidelitous to one person. Many monogamous people fall in love with polyamorous people too, but pursuing a monogamous person, becoming involved with them is not loving.

It is cruel, chaos causing behavior. You are setting the monogamous person up for pain via heartbreak. By asking them to accept you are dating others, you are forcing them into your lifestyle choice. Even if they "love you so much" they insist they "will be okay with it," you are still cruel to allow them to spend all their time, attention and focus on you, when you are not willing to give it all to them in return. This is called cuckolding in the BDSM (Bondage, Domination, Submission, Sadism, and Masochism) community. Some people pick this relationship style on purpose because they enjoy pain, which is why cuckolding is a BDSM option.

If you say you will date them but will "back off" when they find someone else that is also monogamous, you are not freeing them; you are giving them false hope. They cannot date someone else because they are monogamous to you. People who are monogamous won't date others while they are dating you because that is Polyamory. You are their number one person in their monogamous relationship, and they will not find another monogamous relationship until the one with you is over.

That is how monogamous relationships work: the participants are devoted to one person until it's over. To presume there is a monogamous person out there that will date this lover of yours while you are lovers is egotistical because monogamous people aren't interested in people who are currently having sex with someone else.

To believe you can turn a monogamous person into a polyamorous person is egotistical and cruel because the mono will try, out of love for you, to be something they are not. You are using their emotional attachment to you to damage their psyches. Your choices in dating a monogamous person are this:

1.   Change into a monogamous person yourself

2.   Break up with them to remove their hope you will be with just them some day.

There is no difference between dating a married person who has made a monogamous commitment to one person (cheating,) and dating a single monogamous person whose stated lifestyle choice involves one person loving only them and vice versa, to feel happy, safe and confident.

There are exceptions. Some people are "poly-minded," enjoying the theory of a polyamorous lifestyle, but only have time for one love in their lives, for now. There are also people who are happy to have one person in their lives, while their lover has other lovers.

BDSM

BDSM (Bondage, Domination, Submission, Sadism, and Masochism) is often used to work through our childhood trauma. Many people have experienced trauma in life and have yet to feel all the feelings associated with that trauma. Effective, experienced, service oriented Dominants can discover that trauma through extensive interviews, then eventually, after building trust, recreate it safely to allow their submissive to work through those scary feeling they had, knowing they can use their safe word at any moment to stop the activity and work through the feelings with someone to comfort them at hand. Many submissives need to learn to say "No." Some learn to be manipulative instead of learning to say "No".

Dominants can work through their abuses by seeing trauma, and watch it be handled by their submissive. They learn boundaries. The submissive teaches them what appropriate limits are and where abuses should have been stopped. For example, a spanking is a reasonable punishment in childhood, which a submissive can easily endure (even enjoy,) but forced blowjobs are abuse, and that becomes very clear as it's acted out, and stopped.

Dominants get the see their submissives cry and express their pain, and use their power, their "No" or safe word, to stop the abuse. The Dominants have pain bottled up, and the release by the submissive helps the Dominant be vulnerable enough to feel it through their submissive, in a very safe place where they have control. The Dominant learns to let go of pent-up pain, and how to handle it productively. They watch their submissive work through it in a healthy way, by expressing it in a safe place where they have the power to stop it.

This dynamic seems to happen in all relationships where one or both parties were abused in childhood, or in prior relationships. They tend to recreate their abuse, verbal or behavioral (remember neglect is also an abuse) and try to overcome it, by fixing it this time and make it a tolerable memory, that doesn't make them pain every time they think of it. They can rewrite the memory to a gentler one.

The problem with BDSM is that it attracts sadists, sociopaths, and narcissists, who do not want to help you or themselves but simply hurt you for their pleasure. They feel higher when you are in pain. There may be some form of healing for them, but they tend to just use people as an object as if there was nothing going on behind their eyes. Their version of "care" is not damaging a Submissive so much that they are too broken to come back. These folks simply don't want to break their toys.

It is always best to get references about someone before you go off alone to play or "scene" with them, particular references from other submissives, who have already experienced the play style of the Dominant you are interested in. Most submissives will be honest when no other Dominants are around. They don't want the reputation of a tattle-tale in the community. Try asking submissives for advice in the restroom, when all the Dominants have left. Submissives often compare bruises, bragging about them, and their healing, show off their fun clothes, tell stories and gush about their current love, in the privacy of the bathroom. I've had some of the best conversations in my life, in a bathroom. All scenes and play should be negotiated and agreed to ahead of time. Otherwise, it's abuse.

Swinging

Having sex with someone right after you meet them indicates to most people, with a few rare exceptions, that the relationship is just about sex. Sex releases the hormones Dopamine and Serotonin in our brains. These brain chemicals cause us to feel good. For many people, this is their drug of choice. It's all natural and harmless. It can make us feel high for days at a time, and if more people enjoyed it, we would have a far happier planet with less conflict. (If Bonobos can do it, why can't humans?)

Sex can be fun with strangers because of the heightened physical risks, mostly due to not knowing if they are dangerous. Casual sex reduces the need to be vulnerable and is, therefore, safer for your psyche to avoid damage. You cannot have a weak heart if you haven't opened your heart to someone. You are safe from the pain of loss and rejection. It can be fun to have lovers you see on occasion and are friendly with but don't share any responsibilities with, and so have no commitments.

Swinging is easier on the heart and easier to make time for, in our busy lives. The connection to a casual sex partner tends to be less connected. Many people can be "open" and connect to another human for a few minutes while in the heat of passion, or a few minutes telling someone a sad story about themselves, like in a group therapy session, but the vulnerability that comes from admitting mistakes, asking for help, showing up when someone has an emotional crisis, putting yourself out there and making yourself available for pain and rejection, are all not expected or warranted in swinger lifestyle. They want moments of intensity, not the strings of drama that are a natural part of more deeply connected relationships.

Feelings don't get hurt in casual sex relationships. You don't have to explain yourself if you fail to show up, you simply missed a good party. All the trappings of a relationship aren't there; you can relax, enjoy the moment, and not worry about who to call when or why when it's over. You just do what you feel like and no one judges you for it, it's just fun sex with a friend or two. It's not for everyone, but it's okay for you to enjoy it if you do.

Chapter 1. Polyamorous Relationship

In my definition, polyamory is the ability to love (or form deep personal relationships with) more than one individual at a time. It doesn't necessarily mean that the polyamorous individual is always involved with multiple people at once or that all of their relationships are sexual. In fact, I know many people who identify as polyamorous asexual people meaning that while they may love multiple partners, they simply aren't interested in having a sexual relationship with any of them.

As you can tell from the preceding statement, the common myth that all polyamorous people are sex-crazed friends just looking to satisfy their urges isn't true. For some poly people, sex is important but, for others, it may not even be on their radar. Just as monogamous individuals vary greatly in their desire for sexual activity, poly people vary as well. In fact, for most of the polyamorous people that I know personally, they are far more interested in the emotional attachment to others than any physical interaction.

In many cases, a polyamorous household looks more like a bunch of really close friends sharing a home than a Greek orgy, so if you think you want to get into polyamory as a way to set some sexual Olympic record, you are probably reading the wrong book. (Hustler might have some good leads on that subject.)

Now, this isn't to say that some poly people don't engage in sexual activities. I'd honestly say that most of them do and many are very open to discussing sex and everything related to it. If you get a group of polyamorous people together, assuming they aren't all asexual, the discussion will eventually lead to talking about sex but, then again, doesn't the same thing happen with monogamous people? The only real difference is that the polyamorous people may be talking about more than one partner while the monogamous people won't.

Poly people are also more likely to talk openly about the important things like the number of partners, sexual safety, STD testing and full disclosure because they aren't inhibited by the sexual taboos that prevent most monogamous people from discussing these things. Sex can be a dangerous thing with so many sexually transmitted diseases around today.

Unfortunately, monogamous individuals are often hesitant to fully disclose their sexual histories because they have been conditioned by society to think that having too many partners or participating in certain behaviors makes them undesirable or unclean. This leads to the spread of STD's because people don't get tested or they don't share enough information for their sexual partners to protect themselves. In a poly circle, people are usually very willing to discuss their sexual histories, the safety measures they consider absolute necessities and, in some cases, the poly community even assists its own by sharing bad experiences to keep the same thing from happening to others. As you can see, this up-front and fully disclosed discussion can offer some advantages.

As we mentioned before, the poly household often looks like a bunch of friends sharing a house because that's often, exactly, what it is. For example, in a poly triad (three poly people who are together), you might find two women who are :

a) each involved with the male of the group but not each other

b) one man and one woman who are each involved with a second woman but not each other

c) two men involved with one woman but not each other

d) all of them involved with each other. If they all live in one house, they may share meals, expenses, obligations, and rooms.

Conversely, they might all live in different parts of the country and only get together occasionally or communicate online. While it is hoped that all members of the triad are friendly and amiable towards each other, there have certainly been poly triads where two members who were not romantically linked to one another didn't even like the other individual. In a molecule (a group of linked poly people) anything can happen. The wonderful thing about polyamory is that it isn't governed by the rules and conventions that most monogamous people think of when it comes to love and relationships. Since we are already on the fringe, it is okay to make our path and find the love we want, rather than the love society tries to mold us into accepting.

In the modern world, polyamory is important because there just isn't enough love in the world. Everywhere you look, you see hate, prejudice, and pain. Wouldn't it be nice to see people who care about each other and who work towards common goals? One of the points that stood out to me the most when I first discovered the poly community is that these people genuinely care about the world and most of them are very sensitive to its plight. They want to see things get better because they are tired of seeing all the pain. Being willing to share their love with as many people as possible just helps them to reach that goal. Love doesn't diminish from being shared, but it can expand to fill even the darkest of recesses when it is allowed to grow.

As a polyamorous person, I can tell people I love them and mean it, even platonically, without feeling like I am taking something away from my partner. Sometimes, those three words can be the most powerful message in the world. Those words can make the difference between someone fighting to get back on their feet or just giving up and letting the world turn them cold. I can hug a friend and not have to worry that my partner is going to be angry about it. (How many monogamous men can say that? Yes, jealousy exists in the poly world too, but it's usually handled differently.)

Pansexual

To go a bit further, in my personal experience, I've always known there were some things I couldn't give to a partner and, being pansexual; one partner couldn't provide everything I was looking for. Polyamory allows me to say I love you enough that I want you to be happy and I can trust you enough to let you find that happiness without fear of losing you. Polyamory makes you step back and realize that a relationship is not ownership and that your partner is with you because they want to be and not because some social standard dictates that they have to be. Much like the three words, I love you; the realization that someone keeps coming back to you because they want to be with you is a powerful thing.

Lifestyle Choice?

That's a big question, and I'm glad you asked. Personally, I know people on both sides of the fence with this discussion, and it has been debated with a lot of heat from either side. I can give you a definite answer to the question. Are you ready for it? Here it comes. The answer is: I don't KNOW. Neither does anyone else.

For some people, yes, it seems to be a choice they have made after reaching an age to make those decisions for themselves. Perhaps through a shared experience, an attempt to revitalize or something else entirely, these folks just decided to give polyamory a try one day and discovered it just felt right. Some of them jump on and off the bandwagon a dozen times. Some try it once, decide it's not for them and that's okay too.

For others, it is something they knew they had wanted before they were even old enough to know what polyamory was. For myself, I fall into the second group. As I got older, experienced life and learned a few things, I discovered there was a word for what I knew all along. As a polyamorous pansexual man, my capacities for love are pretty much wide open. I don't care what gender you are or you were, if love is there, it is there. I know many poly people who feel the same way, and that makes me proud to be a member of the poly community. Is it a lifestyle choice or something you're just born with? Who cares? If it feels right for you, do it. If it doesn't, then don't. It's that simple.

One of the biggest things poly people get tired of hearing from monogamous people is "that's cheating." Poly is anti-cheating, and I'll tell you why. Remember earlier when we mentioned full disclosure and open discussions? Poly people will hold you to it. My rule with every partner has been, "If you are going to do something, do it but be honest about it. Lying is cheating. If you are honest, we are good." Let's repeat that louder for the ones in the back of the class. Lying and Cheating are bad. Honesty is good. Always be honest.

For example, if Frank says he and his wife are poly and she's okay with him meeting others, but then no one ever meets Frank's wife, people are going to be a bit suspicious. Sorry but that is the way it is. We've learned as a community that sometimes people lie to get what they want so we protect ourselves by adding that healthy layer of suspicion to hedge ourselves from getting hurt.

If someone did meet up with Frank and found out his wife wasn't cool about it, you can bet the local poly community is going to find out pretty quick that Frank was less than truthful. As a rule, polyamorous people have very big hearts, so we hate being lied to and we respect other people's feeling and emotions. Quite simply, if we wouldn't want someone to do it to us, why would we do it to them? Poly people aren't perfect but, as a rule, they are honest and sensitive to the emotional impacts of their actions upon others. Let's say it again because it's so important. Lying is bad. Honesty is good.

To go a bit further, poly people are also very big on maintaining open and honest discussions with their polycule and prospects. A lot of poly people live quietly without spreading too much information to friends and family to avoid confrontation but, within their polycule, the conversations are much more in-depth. We all know how easy it is for two people to have a misunderstanding. Couples get divorced every day over the most minimal issues. Now imagine three or more people all involved in a relationship. It becomes vital to discuss feelings, perceptions and emotional impacts of every member of the polycule or the whole unit can dissolve quickly.

If a new member is being added to the polycule or if someone decides to leave it, it can reconfigure the whole group while trying to arrange for the scheduling and emotional needs of each member. In most cases, if a poly person is dating you and they decide to inform you that they are polyamorous, it's because they are seriously interested in you and want to know how you would fit into their ideal of a polycule or if you would even be a candidate. (PRO TIP: If you got the "let's talk about your thoughts on polyamory" discussion, we probably really, really, really like you. If it's not your cup of tea, we understand but let us down gently.

Chapter 2. Understanding Polyamorous

Some call it "group marriage," which is impossible, of course, since no government (yet) recognizes such a thing. Still, others prefer the term "tribes."

It's like polygamy and polyandry and swinging, but more complicated. In polyfidelity, you can have all manner of pairings (guy-guy, girl-girl, and guy-girl) which allow for group sex. But there's a catch. You can only have sex within your closed circle. Having sex outside that group is cheating. For this to work, everyone in that tribe obviously has to get along.

The advantage of this is that so long as everyone sticks to the rules, and so long as they all have a medical check-up before signing on, they can have multiple partners without the risk of contracting an STD. There are many variations of polyfidelity. The Kerista Village movement in San Francisco tried it out from 1971 to 1991, maintaining a purely heterosexual community. They shared resources and property and lived like a large family before they split up. Some remain "married," but their numbers are now smaller.

Geometric Relationships
There are various types of poly-exclusive relationships. The most common one is called a "geometric relationship." In some cases, these are essentially modern terms for polygamy or polyandry.

Triads
This usually involves a legally married couple who live with a third person. Often, that third person is considered to be a spouse (as was the case with my Gūmā – paternal aunt) and shares the man's bed. I'm told that some Mormon families who still practice polygamy (despite the ban on it), prefer this term to avoid problems with the federal law.

Vs
Also spelled "vee," this again involves three people, but they don't have to be married. In a V relationship, one is the hinge, while the

other two are adjuncts. A typical V pairing involves a man and two women, or one woman and two men. Vs are usually temporary because two members have a stronger bond and were already together when the third person entered the relationship.

Quads

Quads usually involve two legally married couples who live together as a single family unit. Not only do they share a home and all the responsibility that entails (including rearing children), but they also share each other's beds. While most quads are heterosexual couples, other sexual pairings also exist.

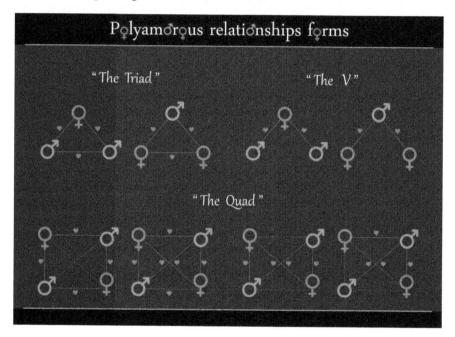

Ns

Ns again involves two couples (not necessarily married and not necessarily heterosexual), but it's complicated, so please bear with my diagram. In an N relationship, you have Person A who's with Person B, and Person C who's with Person D. With me so far?

The thing is, Person A has strong feelings for Person C, which are reciprocated. Since Person B wants their partner to be happy, ditto with person D, they're fine with A and C getting it on. In some cases, B and D get it on, as well.

16

What makes Ns different from Quads is that A has no interest in D (at least not in that way) and B has no interest in C.

Mono-Poly (or Mono/poly)
This is the one my Tàipó (great-grandmother) had. After having eleven children, she was fed up with sex. Since my great grandfather went on to sire five more children with Gūmā, it was clear he wasn't fed up with it yet. In fact, family rumor has it that we have far more blood relatives in California than we know about.

Monopolies are relationships where one partner has no interest in playing around, but their partner does. What makes monopolies different from marriages or partnerships with a cheating other half? In a monopoly, the monogamous one knows about and is fine with the partner who likes to play around. Quite a lot, actually, but I feel those about cover the gamut. The rest are mere variations of those I've already cited.

The point I've tried to make in this section is that fidelity, faithfulness, and loyalty does not necessarily have to be limited to one other person. In some cultures, polygamy and polyandry are the norms. This doesn't mean those cultures are peopled by sexually depraved beings. Only that they have different standards.

Some define "traditional" marriage as a bond between one man and one woman only. Others suggest that without this exclusive pairing, chaos will ensue. Most who spout such nonsense have never traveled farther than the nearest mall or 7-11. Or if they have, they never strayed beyond the guided tours.

Ours is a diverse world with equally diverse concepts of what qualifies as "traditional", "right", "normal" and "proper". The same certainly applies to the concept of relationships, as well as to what constitutes fidelity.

Getting to know Polyamory and Open Relationships
"Amor", love, is the key word here and explains why some who embrace the poly lifestyle look down on swingers. Poly people, like monogamists, also seek intimacy, companionship, and love. Yes, love. It's just that they don't equate love with the physical act of sex. You might want to read that last line again.

Polyamorous people are capable of romantic sentiments and can be fiercely loyal to their partners. They can stand by them no matter what and sacrifice a lot for the good of their mates. They can also have their hearts broken. But they also see the sexual act as both a biological function as well as a human need. As such, the fulfillment of that need is not seen as a compromise of what they feel toward their partners.

To poly people, sexual commitment to just one person is suffocating. It's like being told they can't talk to someone else, hang out with their old friends, talk or look at someone of the opposite sex (or the same in the case of gays and lesbians), can't touch another human being, can't smile at someone, can't befriend another, etc. They don't believe that having sex with others in any way, shape, or form mitigates their love for their partner. This is the same argument that swingers espouse—which makes the polyamorous rather hypocritical in their disdain, don't you think?

Some even go so far as to suggest that polyamory is a sexual orientation, like being straight, gay, or bi. There is an international polyamorous movement, and their values are as follows:

• Faith and loyalty are about who you commit to and wish to spend the rest of your life with. A polyamorous person is therefore open about their sexual needs with their partner and does not engage in secret relationships. When sleeping with others, they take great care to practice safe sex so as not to infect themselves and their partners.

• Negotiation and agreement are about compromise and understanding that not all are comfortable with open relationships. Polyamorous people, therefore, agree to certain conditions with their partners (especially those who are monogamous). This includes letting their primary partners know about their other relationships.

• Boundaries are important because even the polyamorous see the value of living and acting within a specific framework. The practice of safe sex is part of those boundaries.

• Respect and dignity mean that the polyamorous respect the dignity of all their partners, sexual and otherwise. It also means that they respect to gender and sexual preferences regardless of their sexual orientation.

- Non-possessiveness is the view that no one can own another, nor impose unrealistic or unreasonable demands that limit them. Jealousy and possessiveness are therefore seen as responses to be explored and understood, and if possible, avoided.

Chapter 3. Loving Without Limits

The problem with most couples is that they've succumbed to the romantic poet's idea of "the soulmate" and that is, out of billions of people in this world, there is only one person out there who can make you happy. But what are the odds? What if this "soulmate" lives on the other side of the ocean? What if "the one" happens to be gay? Or married? Or dead?

If we were to entrust everything to serendipity, then we'd all end up as spinsters and perpetual bachelors. Thus, we go on settling for partners who fall just a bit short from our idea of a "perfect mate." Over time, discontent inevitably develops as differences between personalities, goals, and desires become more and more apparent.

Nature designed us to be on the constant lookout for reproductive opportunities. We may love someone and promise to stick with that person, but that doesn't stop that instinctive part of yourself from being drawn to others. While some people are hard-wired for monogamy, others aren't. And while there is nothing wrong with monogamous relationships, polyamorous relationships provide people with an opportunity to be true to one's nature and one's partner without the burden of shame and guilt.

Before you think of it, no, polyamory is not about appeasing the guilt of justifying affairs. Instead, it's about preserving your relationship by preventing dissatisfaction and preserving your idea of your significant other as a suitable mate. This brings us to the next benefit…

Polyamorous Relationships Last Longer

Surprisingly, the reason why most marriages don't last is that of a series of small personal differences which tend to accumulate over time until it finally takes its toll. She doesn't want to go to a football game with him. He doesn't want to go shopping with her. He/she doesn't want to try out this new sex position. He/she then doubts the idea of his/her partner as a suitable mate.

What if he finds a lover who loves football as much as he does? What if she finds a lover who enjoys shopping? What if he/she finds a lover who shares his/her sexual fantasies? Would you then deprive your partner of that happiness?

People in polyamorous relationships don't hold each other back from finding a soulmate in different people. They don't prevent and begrudge each other from feeling satisfaction and achieving a sense of completeness through others. They don't hinder each other from seeing and experiencing joy and love and beauty in others because they want what's best for their partner/s. They can be happy with each other, and they can be happy for each other. When you come to think of it, polyamorous love is the most loving, most selfless kind of love there is.

Polyamory prevents unnecessary pain.

When people in monogamous relationships eventually feel a sense of discontent, they end up doing one of these things:

- Break up

- Suffer silently and make each other unhappy

- Have affairs

The thing about needs is that they change constantly. What you may need right now may not be what you need fifteen years from now. When you're in a polyamorous relationship, you don't need to go through a painful breakup with someone that you've cherished for years just because you've found someone who can satisfy your current needs. You don't have to hurt other people by dragging them into a rollercoaster ride of your drama.

Furthermore, open relationships reduce the occurrence of infidelity and the guilt that comes along with it. Because there was consent all throughout, the people involved don't feel that they've been duped and their egos are less likely to be wounded. There is no temptation to "seek revenge" because the participants know fully well that they, too, can love others whenever they wish to.

Polyamorous Relationships Are Stronger

Polyamorous relationships are organized on trust and effective communication, something that's lacking even in monogamous marriages. If one were to describe the communication in a polyamorous relationship in one word, that word would be relentless. After all, this is the only way to make sure that the needs of everyone involved are satisfactorily met. Polyamorous lovers make sure that each partner feels loved and appreciated. No one must feel neglected or left out. This means polyamorous partners are willing to invest a great deal of time and energy, two very important ingredients to the success of any relationship.

The thing about polyamorous relationships is that the participants recognize that the love they feel for one partner is unique from the love they feel for another partner. These types of love may be felt in varying degrees, but you value all of them equally. You don't treat your partners like they are interchangeable. You treat each partner as someone who is irreplaceable and amazing in his/her way.

Polyamory helps you become a better person

Apart from learning to love selflessly, you can develop your capacity to embrace diversity. Polyamorous relationships provide you with greater learning opportunities from each lover that you take. More importantly, you become free from the society's cookie cutter pattern for relationships. You learn to trust in your internal sense of correctness. Simply put, you gain emotional maturity.

Polyamorous relationships are more sexually satisfying

A monogamous sexual relationship limits your perception of sex and hinders you from realizing what you might be doing wrong in the bedroom. As we've repeatedly pointed out in this book, polyamory is not about promiscuity. It's not a permit to have sex with anyone and everyone. That said, one of the benefits you'll receive from polyamorous relationships is a broader range of sexual knowledge and new sensations owed to the varied experiences of other partners.

Ultimately, in a polyamorous relationship, there is more love, more happiness, more resources, and more perspectives available to everyone. Parents in polyamorous relationships are grateful for lovers who lend a helping hand in raising their kids. Couples in polyamorous relationships benefit from the experience, the insight, and the strengths of their other lovers. Day-to-day chores are divided in the household. There are more people to help in problem-solving, thus, reducing stress. More people love you and support you in your dreams in life. In the long run, this will improve your physical and mental health.

Love

Whether you're new to polyamorous relationships or trying it on to see if it fits, it is important to be able to understand the different terms associated with it.

First, we start with terms about the different types of polyamorous relationships. Even though the rules and the organization depend entirely on the parties involved, the most common models for polyamorous relationships are as follows:

- Primary Model

- Multiple Primary Partners Model

- Multiple Non-Primary Model

Primary refers to the chief members in the hierarchy of a multi-person arrangement. The primary couple is the one with the strongest bond. They may be married or unmarried. Either way, they are open to developing new relationships with others. Even so, they agree that their relationship takes precedence over any other affairs. This means they place the majority of their time and effort on their relationship while their relationship with other people receives less time and less energy. In most arrangements, primary couples live together in the same house.

Sometimes, co-primaries (primary couples) demand emotional fidelity from each other. That is, they are free to engage in external sexual relationships, but it must be limited to physical intimacy only.

There is also a type of relationship called geographical non-monogamy wherein the co-primaries have agreed to have sexual relationships with other people only while they are apart.

A veto is an agreement in a relationship where one of the co-primaries possesses the power to restrict his/her lover's freedom to engage in other relationships. This includes limiting specific sexual practices with the satellite partners or the secondary partners.

The advantage of this model is that its living arrangements are the closest to being conventional. There is also greater security between the primary couples because they know that in the end, they are each other's priority. The disadvantage is the unpredictability of satellite relationships. Despite the limits imposed, there is always the danger of developing a deeper attachment with the secondary partners. Furthermore, problems may occur when the secondary individuals demand equal rights and attention.

Secondary refers to a person/s that is a part of a multiple-arrangement relationship without any legal, economic, or emotional complexities involved. Less is expected from a secondary partner regarding commitment.

Multiple Primary Partners
For couples who find that primary and secondary set-ups are hard to work out, the multiple primary partners model is an option. In this type of polyamorous arrangement, three or more people are considered as primaries, and they all have an equal say when it comes to the relationship. They also have equal responsibilities when it comes to time, energy, commitment, finances, sex, and others.

Polyfidelity
This is a subtype of the Multiple Primary Partners model wherein three to six consenting adults are bound together in a group marriage. They live under the same roof (cohabitation) and divide responsibilities among themselves. These include kids, finances, chores, etc. Thus they become a poly family. Such families are also referred to as a cellular family. Cellular families, however, need not necessarily reside under one roof. Instead, they may choose to live near each other.

They also have sexual relations with each other and can have kids with all of the persons involved. If members are heterosexual, all women are allowed to make love with the men and vice versa. If all members are bisexual, they may all make love with each other. Bisexual individuals who are polyamorists are sometimes referred to as bipolar. The term panamory is defined as a capacity to feel romantic or sexual love for different partners regardless of gender. Thus, a straight woman can be capable of loving a gay man sexually in her way.

The word "fidelity" is included in the term because members of this relationship model agree to become exclusive with each other. Therefore, they cannot have relationships with other people outside their party. This set-up is also called a closed group marriage. If they do fall in love with someone outside the party, the others must decide whether or not to allow the outsider to enter their group. The very opposite of this is called an open network where members are free to add new lovers as they please.

When all members of a group marriage regard each other as equals regarding rights and duties, the arrangement is called a democratic family.

A complex marriage is a term used to describe an arrangement wherein each time a male member joins a group; he is then considered as wedded to all the female members. Likewise, when a female member enters the group, she is then considered as wedded to all the male members.

Men in a group marriage who share a wife are referred to as co-husbands and women who share a husband are called co-wives.

A cluster marriage is quite different in the sense that it involves two or more married couples who move in with other married couples. They are then free to exchange partners. When one member of a couple has relations with a member of another couple, this is called cross-coupling.

A four-cornered marriage refers to a group marriage where there are exactly four members (two couples).

A free mate is a term used to refer to an unmarried member who joins a group relationship.

In a corporate marriage, the individuals agree to a group marriage by registering their union as a legal corporation. Hence, they write down the terms of their obligations including financial duties.

One of the advantages of this relationship model is the pooling of resources. The challenge, on the other hand, is in arriving at a unanimous decision every single time even with the most trivial matters. Accordingly, this type of relationship entails an exceptionally high degree of compatibility between members. In this kind of set-up, cooperation and communication are crucial.

Multiple Non-Primary Relationship
A polyfidelity relationship requires a great amount of time and effort. So what about individuals who cannot offer these? This is where multiple non-primary relationships come in. Individuals are free to engage in an intimate sexual relationship without the constraints associated with a primary set-up. The lovers see each other when they can. This is a viable option for individuals whose lifestyles are too busy to accommodate a primary relationship. The participants may even be married to other people who consent to the idea of them forming extramarital relationships. An open marriage refers to any marriage structure where couples are permitted to have external sexual relations.

Solo poly refers to a polyamorous approach where a single individual does not seek couple-centric relationships. Instead, he/she employs autonomy in selecting lovers without having to ask someone for permission. He/she has a freedom to control the flexibility of the relationships.

Friends with benefits (FWB) pertain to relationships where two or more individuals form a bond of friendship and then engage in sexual activity. However, they do not develop any romantic feelings for each other. They also limit their expectations of each other.

The drawback to this relationship model is when one of the non-primary partners begins wanting more. An example is when one retires or when one's husband/wife suddenly dies. They may suddenly find more time on their hands and begin seeking a primary relationship.

Free love refers to the philosophy that love must not be limited by the concept of commitment or marriage. This is quite different from Abundant Love which is a belief that people are capable of loving one person at a time.

In a triad scenario, a polyamorous relationships that involve three people, members of a triad may be called a trouple. A marriage a Trois is a term used to describe an arrangement where one individual is married to two partners.

A Vee is a triad relationship where one person is sexually related to two persons, but the other two are not romantically involved with each other. This is different from a Delta where all three persons have romantic/sexual relationships with each other.

In a quad scenario, a polyamorous relationship that involve four people, any of the members may or may not have sexual relations with each other.

Agamy is a state of being indifferent to the idea of matrimony or reproduction. Meanwhile, an asexual individual is someone who has no desire for sexual relations or activities but may still become a part of a polyamorous relationship. A Sapiosexual relationship occurs when the connection between polyamorous lovers are based on intelligence rather than sexual attraction.

Bigamy pertains to a relationship wherein a man/woman is married to two females/males.

Polygamy, on the other hand, means being married to multiple spouses at one time. When a woman is wedded to multiple husbands at the same time, it is called polyandry. When a man is wedded to multiple wives at the same time, it is called polygyny.

Adelphogamy is also known as Fraternal Polyandry. It is a polyamorous practice where a group of brothers is all married to one female.

A Line Marriage is a kind of group marriage where younger members are continuously added as the senior members get older. The purpose is to maintain equilibrium as the aging partners will be replaced when they pass on.

You will discover more terms used in polyamorous relationships as we move on to discussing the problems frequently encountered by poly folk and how to approach them.

Chapter 4. Different Types Of Polyamory

As you can tell, polyamory is fairly inclusive of anyone who wants to claim it. Some individuals are asexual, straight, lesbian, gay, bisexual, transgender and every other variation you can think of. It's a pretty open club, and membership doesn't cost a thing.

Something you might not have known though is that there is such a thing as solo polyamory. In the typical instance, solo polyamory can refer to an individual who is polyamorous with multiple relationships yet chooses to live independently of all of their partners.

Also, some people who label themselves as a monopoly are polyamorous individuals who may have a partner who is not polyamorous. Now, hopefully, if a poly person is in a loving relationship with a partner, they can work things out where the needs of both individuals are met but, sometimes, a polyamorous person will stay in a monogamous relationship for various reasons. It has certainly been done with various levels of success over the years and, if that works for them, who has a right to judge their choices? Sometimes, the non-poly partner will agree to let the poly individual pursue their needs outside of the relationship to meet their emotional needs.

The polyunsaturated individual may not have any partner at all and be seeking to find new partners. This nickname of sorts is primarily a slang term used in areas where openness about sexuality and gender are often eschewed. In a world where people have been modified to accept and perpetuate monogamy, it can be difficult for a polyamorous person to find other poly people, let alone compatible partners.

A polycule is a network of individuals who are connected through their partners with some mutual sharing partners or all partners in some cases.

That leads us back to the point in the last chapter, the "let's talk about your thoughts on polyamory" discussion. A polyamorous person is likely to have this discussion several times in their life and, no surprise, it is a scary subject to broach. You remember trying to talk to your crush in high school? The picture is telling them that you like them, but you want to see other people too and to hope the message doesn't get mistranslated. (ANOTHER PRO TIP: Sometimes, "I think we should see other people" isn't the end of a relationship but if you are planning to have this talk with someone, especially a spouse, you might want to choose your phrasing carefully to avoid hurt feelings - and alimony payments).

Personally, I've always been the up-front, tell it like it is type, so I pretty much let people know who I am early in the relationship. That may or may not work well for you, but it has served me well. I find it weeds out the ones who aren't the slightest bit interested in poly right off the bat, so it saves me time and frustration later. Something along the lines of "I like you, and I don't want either of us to get hurt down the road so can I explain something and get your thoughts?" is a great conversation starter. It gets their attention, reassures them that you are interested in them and creates a path for an open dialog. Where you go from there is up to you but, in my experience, people who truly care about you are going to be pretty receptive to what you have to say.

Long Distance Blues

Earlier we mentioned that not all polycules could live together. Sometimes due to finances, employment or other reasons, the individual members of a molecule may be separated by great distances. In these situations, communication, trust and honesty become even more important.

The old saying is "absence makes the heart grow fonder" and, fortunately, that can be very true but, in some cases, it also cools the fires of romance too. A polycule member who feels left out and isolated may decide they are no longer needed or wanted. A long distance member of a triad that is seeing a couple might begin to feel jealousy or resentment for the couple having time together without them. I've seen it happen many, many times and it's usually because someone got busy or just forgot to take a few extra minutes to stay in contact.

Think of your polycule as a rare exotic plant. It requires attention every day to remain healthy and vibrant. If you forget to water the plant too many times, it withers. Your phone calls, texts or instant messages are like the water to your polycule relationships. If you let them dry up, you are going to start seeing signs of trouble fairly quickly.

To avoid this, take a few minutes each day or at least every other day to send your partners a message that you are thinking about them and that you still care. It might be something as easy as a text message; a picture shared to their Facebook wall or a voicemail left, so they will hear it when they get off work.

If you say you are going to talk to them at a particular time, do it. It's frustrating when we have to wait for someone, and if they are late or a no show, it can be even worse. Why would you do that to someone you care about? Of course, there will be times when it is unavoidable but, for the most part, you should be able to schedule in a few minutes for a personal chat. If not, you may need to re-evaluate your priorities if you want to sustain the relationship.

Remember there are a thousand methods to say I love you. It might be reminding them to pick up their anxiety medication from the pharmacy or sending them a picture or two throughout the day. It could be a birthday card or a surprise anniversary visit. Be creative. Let your heart lead, and you will find that love has many languages which can span any distance.

Be reassuring. It's scary being away from the people we love. We worry about them. We worry that they will find someone better than us. We worry that they already did and they don't know how to tell us. We just worry that we worry too much. That's why it's important to reassure your long distance loves that they are still very important to you and very much a part of your life.

Just because your partner is living under the same roof, it doesn't mean the problems magically go away either. I've personally known many couples who thought they would try polyamory as an experiment and wound up divorced or unhappy with each other. The cause every single time? Lack of communication.

It's easy to remember that we have to maintain the long distance relationships because we don't see that person every day. We miss them. The one who just left the toilet seat up and the dirty socks on the living room floor, however, sometimes we wish he would go away for a while. We tend to bicker with that one. We don't always communicate from a place of love and caring. We forget that they are sensitive and have emotional needs too and, then, we wind up in relationship trouble.

For example, I recently talked to a friend who told me he had his wife and his girlfriend living with him. He loves them both. The polyamorous are awesome. Still, when you have a polyamorous every night, it becomes routine, and then one on one love making becomes something special. He needed to have some alone time with each of the women in his life, but he didn't want to hurt either of them by asking for it. I pointed out to him that, if he was feeling this way, wasn't it likely that they felt it too? He hadn't stopped to think about it from that angle and, when he did, it was like a huge burden was lifted. He knew what he needed to do. He needed to communicate openly with both of them so they could all get their needs met.

Another problem with having our poly partners under one roof is New Relationship Energy (NRE) anxiety and jealousy. NRE is common. Even the monogamous folks will understand this one. It's that "butterflies in your stomach, walking on clouds, love them so much, they are perfect" feeling that we get when we find a new love. Six months down the road, it's usually "she snores and squeezes the toothpaste tube wrong" but, for now, you are certain that they are an angel made of gold and you want to spend every waking moment with them. That's great. Good for you.

Someone else was here first, and she wants some of your time too. She's been there for years and, yes, she may squeeze the toothpaste tube wrong and snore, but she loves you even though you steal the covers and fart in your sleep. She is happy for you that you found someone that makes you happy. That's call compersion, and she's got a lot of that. Unfortunately, she's also got anxiety. Is this new love so perfect that you won't want her anymore? When will she get some of your time and attention? When was the last time you looked at her like that? Not long after that, jealousy comes creeping in. She's certain you are through with her. Your late night calls to your new love used to be your time to spend with her.

Once again, communication is the key. Polyamory is much like a finely tuned dance. If we keep all the lines of communication open, no one feels pushed out or left behind. Miss a step and the whole dance falls into chaos and disorder. So, we have to find the balance. We have to be willing to say, hey, new love energy is great, but this long term love is pretty fabulous too. Surprise her with breakfast in bed and pick up your socks off the living room floor. She'll be reassured that you still care and your home life is going to go a lot smoother. She might even enjoy talking to you about your new love interest as well because someone who is important to you will likely be a special person to her too. After all, they both love you, so they share something in common. If you are really lucky, she will even remember this lesson when her time rolls around to find NRE, and she'll be there to reassure you too because these emotions visit us all.

Now, I'm going to take a little sideways jaunt to make a note here because I think it is very important. I know not everyone will agree with me, but that's okay. You see I have a personal problem with the old, green-eyed monster, Jealousy. I think it is an ugly and useless emotion. I will admit, in my younger days, I had a bit of jealousy, and sometimes it got me in over my head but, as I aged and mellowed, I learned something. Jealousy is rarely a productive thing. Most of the time, it breeds destruction. It can ruin a relationship because you start seeing things that aren't even there. I've finally reached the point where I don't feel jealousy anymore and, more often than not, I find it disturbing when I see it in other people. Some folks find it cute when their partners get all puffed up and jealous because they see it as the person cares. Personally, I see it as you don't trust me and you think our relationship has become ownership. Why do I mention all this?

Simply, because, as much as jealousy irritates me, it is usually a sign that something is needing to be fixed in the relationship. It's also a warning to folks who are just venturing into poly waters: many of the people who have been around poly for years have developed a similar feeling towards jealousy and, sometimes, their way of fixing the relationship issue is simply to end it. Most polyamorous people are extremely reasonable and sensitive to their partner's feelings but, if you make a continuous display of jealous behavior, they may quickly tire of jumping through hoops to appease you.

Chapter 5. Polyamory And Its Problems

What are the problems usually encountered by polyamorists?

Jealousy
Some poly folks tend to suffer from Exclusion Jealousy. This pertains to an irrational fear of being left behind by a lover when he/she embraces a new partner.

To prevent jealousy in a polyamorous relationship, you must develop a clear and open pathway of communication. Sit down together and establish rules that state what one is and isn't allowed to do. If you doubt whether you can stick with a certain rule or not then tell your partner/s from the very beginning. Say: "No, I don't think I can be happy as a secondary partner." Likewise, if you want to hold on tighter to your existing partner, then set firmer guidelines.

Another thing you must keep in mind to prevent jealousy is time management. If you've agreed to become a part of a democratic poly family, then make sure that you devote your time and energy equally among the members of your family. Yes, you're allowed to have your favorites, but that doesn't mean you have to make everyone else feel less special. It's a lot like having children. You have a responsibility to love them all the same.

You must learn to manage your expectations in the first place. When you're in a poly relationship, you can't expect to do everything together. Otherwise, one of you is bound to feel suffocated. Some poly folk makes the mistake of thinking that obtaining a common lover will result in an equal arrangement. You may get jealous when you see that your partners are starting to develop a stronger bond with each other. It's inevitable. Some connections grow faster than others, and you can't control chemistry. Just remember that while your partner may find a "soulmate" in a new lover, you are also free to find your own "soulmate" in another lover. Lastly, if the arrangement is bothering you, don't be afraid of putting your foot down. Tell your lover/s what's making you unhappy or uncomfortable.

In the early phase of the polyamorous relationship, most individuals experience a certain "high" from NRE (New Relationship Energy). This is an overwhelming sense of infatuation brought about by the thrill of the new relationship. NRE can last for years. This is due to the rush of vasopressin and oxytocin in the system. That said, there is also what is called the ORE (Old Relationship Energy) between long-time lovers. Compared to NRE, it is more stable, more lasting and more capable of providing feelings of comfort. When entering in a polyamorous relationship, it is the lovers' job to cherish and nurture both energies.

The best solution to combating jealousy is to develop your capacity for Compersion. This refers to your ability to experience joy on behalf of your partner when he/she takes pleasure from a relationship outside your own. The worst thing that you can do is to ask your lover to stay away from the person that he/she has learned to love.

Insecurity
Another issue that affects those who are considering polyamory is the idea of their lovers comparing them with the other lovers. Observing the similarities and differences between one's lovers is inevitable. Therefore, if you wish to be a part of a polyamorous relationship, then you must first establish a healthy relationship with yourself. This includes boosting your self-confidence. Be aware of your assets and nurture them. That said, you mustn't consider satellite lovers as competition. Instead, learn to accept the fact that you are different and that each of you has something unique to offer. After all, this diversity is the reason why you and your partner/s chose to pursue polyamory in the first place.

Learn to look at comparisons in a different light. See it as a way to highlight each other's uniqueness and as a recognition of the exceptional value/s which each of you adds to the relationship.

It's important that you don't treat your relationships as isolated affairs. Involve your partner/s in your relationships and involve yourself in your partner/s relationships. Get to know your partner/s lover/s. Learn who they are as human beings, and you'll eventually learn to appreciate them and see what your partner/s saw in them in the first place.

Members of a polyamorous group relationship should strive to build each other's self-esteem by providing each other with genuine compliments and appreciating each other's efforts.

Communication Problems
In making decisions that will affect the relationship, be sure to involve all members of the triad/quad/poly family. Talk directly to each of your lovers instead of asking one of your partners to relay the info to another. Likewise, refrain from believing in related information. Instead, go directly to the source.

Unrealistic Expectations
Don't use polyamory as a way to solve problems in an existing relationship. Don't start a new relationship until you can fix all of your issues with one partner. Draw contracts to clarify to all parties involved the possibility (or impossibility) of marriage in the future. There are instances when two members decide to go in a monogamous relationship. In this case, let them go and wish them well.

Remember that a polyamorous relationship must develop an increased capacity to love and be loved. Therefore, if love is lacking in an existing relationship, there's no guarantee that you'll find it in a new one. Don't force any of your relationship/s to be what they aren't. Instead, allow it to be. Find contentment and pleasure in watching your relationship/s bloom into something wonderfully unexpected.

Being a Responsible Lover
What are the rules to follow when engaging in a polyamorous relationship?

Respect your partner/s and their partner/s. Apart from trust and honesty, compassion is another essential virtue in polyamorous relationships. Even when you don't get what your partner/s see in his/her chosen lover/s, trust them to know their feelings.

Set clear limits and respect each other's boundaries. Just because you see that one of your partners enjoy doing an activity with one of the other members, that doesn't mean he/she is open to doing it with you. Never force yourself on anyone even when you're part of a poly family.

Accept that not everything is about you. Be in harmony with the fact that your partner/s has his/her relationship/s just as you have your own. Not everything is a reflection of you or your shortcomings. If you don't enjoy dancing as much as your partner and his other lover do, it's not your fault. Just because your partner and her new lover enjoy walks along the beach like you used to, again, this is not about you. We all have our own experiences and our own needs and guess what, it's perfectly alright.

Don't blame it all on polyamory. Some poly folk make the mistake of connecting all relationship problems to the fact that they're polyamorous. That wouldn't be fair. Just like in monogamous relationships, conflict and misunderstandings normally occur. It all comes back to maintaining honesty and open communication. Sit down together with all parties involved, discuss your issues, and find a solution together. Pay attention to each partner/s problems and suggestions. Lay everything on the table. If you're jealous, don't be afraid to say it. Always consider your partner/s before doing something.

Observe proper hygiene. Maintain a healthy lifestyle. Practice birth control. Keep in mind that everything that you do in one relationship may impact your other relationship/s either positively or negatively. Consult your partner/s before making any important life decisions. This goes without saying but doesn't engage in irresponsible sexual behavior that can place you and your partner at risk for acquiring STIs.

Have the balls to pursue polyamory.
Social stigma is one of the major problems faced by poly folk. If you wish to practice your right to love infinitely, then you have to be strong enough for it. Before starting a relationship, determine which areas of your life will be affected (e.g. your job, your position in the religious community, your kids) Then, make a plan on how to deal with it and how to avoid or lessen the negative impact. Clarify your

goals and straighten your priorities. You have to be certain that a polyamorous relationship is what you want. When you're certain that polyamory will make you happy, then it will be easier for you to fight for it.

Won't having multiple partners increase your chances of acquiring sexually transmitted infections?
Sexual health is another reason why members of a polyamorous relationship should communicate effectively with each other. Poly folk talk a lot about sex and safety. Some even draw contracts to state which sexual practices are allowed and not allowed. It is important to be honest about one's sexual history.

Just like in monogamous relationships, individuals in a polyamorous relationship should be educated about STIs and safe sex. Consult with a reproductive health care provider to learn the proper ways of using barriers such as condoms.

A condom contract refers to a formal agreement where unprotected sexual intercourse is to transpire only between the signees. All of these individuals have been previously screened for STIs. The contract also stipulates the conditions under which the members are allowed to exchange bodily fluids.

Some primary couples practice Body Fluid Monogamy wherein activities which involve the exchange of bodily fluids are performed only with each other and not with secondary lovers.

Poly folk must be willing to perform routine STI tests before having unprotected sex. This is done all throughout the relationship.

Examine each other's bodies and genitals before sex. Know what infected hair follicles and genital warts look like. When in doubt, play it safe. Remember that there's no shame in doing this.

Never allow a partner to pressure you into performing fluid bonding (barrier-free sex) with him/her. If he/she does, then you might want to reconsider their presence in your life.

Other safe sex alternatives in polyamorous relationships include parallel play where two or more couples have intercourse only with their exclusive sex partners while being in the same room with the rest of the group. Under no circumstance must the participants touch another's partner in a sexual way. The pleasure they receive is in watching other couples make love (voyeurism).

Another alternative is a cuddle party where cuddling, massaging, and other kinds of loving physical expressions are allowed. However, extreme sexual stimulation such as masturbation and intercourse is forbidden.

Brainstorm with your partner/s to develop creative ways on how you can safely enjoy polyamorous sex. You're bound to come up with some wild and wonderful ideas. After all, more heads are better than two.

Chapter 6. Deciding Whether Or Not It's For You

I've explained the many types of polyamorous relationships out there that you and your partner can explore if you're interested. What I'd now like to do is address the awkward situation in which everything I've described just isn't your thing. Unfortunately, your partner feels otherwise.

Assuming you haven't already dumped him or her, and assuming you still want to stay together, there are a few things you have to bear in mind. The first thing I'd like to reiterate is what I said in the last chapter:

Polyamorists don't equate love with the physical act of sex. That's the key thing right there.

What I'm trying to say is that, unless your partner dumps you for someone else; assuming they say they love you and mean it, it's just that they want to have sex with others; then what you've got there is a polyamorous person.

They do love you. Just not in the way you may approve of. In other words, it's not about you. It's not a rejection of you; it's not because you've suddenly gained weight, or that you snore, or that they don't like your family, etc. For that, they'd dump you outright.

No, no. It's about them. Them. Your partner isn't attacking or criticizing you. They're honest with you because they don't want to do anything sneaky behind your back. The fact that they're even telling you about it is because they still want you in their lives.

Nor does it necessarily mean you suck in bed. You could have a doctorate in the Kama Sutra, but it still doesn't matter. I repeat - it's not about you.

Monogamists are happy with one person; the polyamorous are not. When a polyamorous person falls in love, the romantic desire for a special connection with others doesn't shut off as it does with monogamists.

So when they say that one person doesn't satisfy their needs, it doesn't mean they're spoiled brats who want every desire met, no matter how minor it is. It simply means that their desire for that special intimacy with another cannot be met by one person alone.

It's like being gay or straight. I know that comes across as shocking to you, an attempt to justify cheating lovers, but it's not. I won't get into the science, but some suggest that the brains of genuinely monogamous people are different from genuinely polyamorous people.

That said, some people are just assholes. Cheating lovers and polyamorous people are not the same things. The former just can't keep their pants or skirts on, regardless of the consequences to themselves and others. The latter, on the other hand, is looking for a romantic connection... Again and again and again.

Sometimes, the best option is just to let them go or to walk away.

How to Handle a Polyamorous Relationship
It's possible you've outgrown your current relationship and wanted to move on, but can't or won't for whatever reason. It's even possible that you still love your partner, but that sexual zing is no longer there. Finally, consider the possibility that your partner feels either of the above regarding you. Whatever the case, you owe each other the truth.

I want to make it very obvious that while polyamory has saved some relationships, it has destroyed many others. It takes a certain kind of mindset to be able to share one's partner both on a sexual as well as on an emotional level.

If polyamory is indeed a sexual orientation, that could explain it. In an ideal world, the polyamorists stick to their kind and the monogamists stay together. Unfortunately, our world has never been ideal, now has it?

If you choose to stay in a relationship with a polyamorous person, know it won't be easy. Sometimes, your best option is just to walk away. And if you want to experiment with polyamory, understand that you can't always have your cake and eat it. Your original partner might not be able to take it, so be ready to let go.

But if you choose to give it a shot, you need to consider three important things:

- Understand what kind of polyamorous relationship you're getting into. I've described the various kinds of pairings and the rules that govern them. Open relationships and swinging mean you and your partner have sex with others, but there's no emotional commitment to those others. This is the ideal for those starting out. If you're getting into a polyfidelity relationship, first see how those in the circle relate to each other. They may be great when you're looking at them from the outside, but another matter when you're on the inside looking out.

- Be flexible but know your boundaries, something you should do in a monogamous relationship, as well. The first key lies in understanding that your partner's motives and behavior are not always about you. The other key lies in them understanding the same thing. Nevertheless, you do have a right to have your needs respected. If your open relationship ends up with your partner wanting to move a third person in and you're not fine with that, get ready to either walk away or adapt to that new other.

- Don't assume the problem has to do with polyamory. When problems arise, it's easy to blame the unconventional relationship as the cause. This isn't fair, since monogamous relationships have their problems, too. It's best to deal with the problem specifically, and don't assume it's because of the relationship. Of course, if polyamory is indeed the problem, then that's another matter entirely. How you deal with that issue is up to you.

Chapter 7. Principles

There are some basic things I want to cover before getting into the nitty-gritty of where to look. Here I will discuss the obstacles that you face, who to look for, and how to look. These are general principles that apply to all the avenues you could use to find someone. The difficulty of finding a polyamorous is explained. Two schools of thought on how to approach a potential third are presented. The importance of the third's comfort and having respect for them are discussed. I'll show you how to stand out in a crowd of couples seeking polyamorous. Last, the question of who to approach is debated.

It's Hard

Finding a polyamorous is hard. Most couples are looking for a no-strings-attached (NSA) polyamorous arrangement, and that may be even harder to find.

When a Clueless Couple starts to look, they think it will be easy. "We're sexy," they say to themselves. "We love having sex with each other. Who wouldn't want to have sex with us?"

But you have to remember that few women are actively looking for NSA sex. The man in the couple should think about how much NSA sex he had when he was single. If he's like most men, casual sex wasn't overly available. Maybe it happened once in a while, but it wasn't something he could rely on.

The woman should think about how open to NSA sex she was when she was single. Assuming that she's bisexual, how often did she go on websites looking for a couple to hook up with? Or even a single man or woman to hook up with? How often did she go home with a man she barely knew? What the woman in many couples is looking for in a third is a willingness to do things she wouldn't do herself.

If you've never been a single bisexual woman, try going onto Craigslist's couples seeking females (mw4w) section or an adult dating website. You'll find there is a huge pool of couples looking for single bisexual women, while the reverse is far less common. Among those in the know, the single bisexual female willing to have NSA sex with or date a couple is called a unicorn. The name was chosen because the mythical beast is so beautiful and so precious, but mostly because it's so hard to find.

This is the bad news: finding a third for a couple is even harder than finding a second for a single man. Your pool is limited to bisexual women. You need to have attraction going in three directions instead of two. (That is, instead of Person A being attracted to Person B and B being attracted to A, A needs to be attracted to B and C, B to A and C, and C to A and B.) And you need to find someone sexually open enough to sleep with two people.

The good news is that the reward is the hottest sex you can imagine. Three people in bed – or on a floor, or a kitchen table – offer infinitely more possibilities than two. When you finally have your polyamorous, it will be worth every minute you spent on getting it.

Approaching Your Third
Given that finding a third is hard, approaching a potential third must be done carefully. There are two schools of thought here.

The first says that you should be upfront about what you are looking for. If you're just looking for sex, be clear about it. Don't hold anything back or be dishonest in any way. It may not be immediate, but if you go up to or message enough women, eventually one will be open to having NSA sex with you and your partner.

The second school of reasoning would have you befriend the woman first. Women willing to have NSA sex are rare. They may be open to doing it spontaneously if they're drinking and having fun, but less willing to plan it out in advance. However, if you befriend bisexual women you both find attractive, they will see you as unique people rather than just another couple looking for a polyamorous.

"There are some women out there who are interested in getting dirty with a couple simply because they're physically attractive. I believe that's a very small minority," says blogger Dave in a Polyamorous 101 post. "It's like any dating type situation: people are more likely to want to fuck you (both) if they like you. Duh. What better way for them to like you than to be interesting, be yourself, and be compatible."

So, which school of thought is right? I tend to favor the second, personally. It won't work for everyone, especially if you're looking for a completely NSA experience. If you're not open to making a new friend or having your third join your bed more than once, doing this is not for you.

But since I find sex usually gets better with practice and feels better when you care about the person, it appeals to me more. First times with a new partner can be awkward, especially for a first polyamorous, so I do recommend doing it more than once!

Make sure that it's clear that the polyamorous is for both of you, not just for one partner or the other. One user on Shybi.com notes that "there are a lot of women out there who succumb to their men's fantasies. Weirdly enough a lot of these women don't identify as bi, and often tell me that they are just "looking for a polyamorous" because he wants it. Either that or they have told their partner that they think they like women and he tells her it's a polyamorous or nothing at all."

Using the right method to approach women will help you get your polyamorous more than perhaps any other factor.

Comfort
Making your third feel comfortable is of the utmost importance. Someone who is comfortable will be open to sharing sexual experiences with you, while someone who is not comfortable is likely to turn tail and run away. Even if your polyamorous takes place, a lack of comfort on one person's part can ruin the fun for everyone involved.

As an example, messaging a random girl online with naked pictures will not make her feel comfortable. As attractive as you and your partner may be, your potential third will want to see your faces first. After some talking back and forth, you can share your nudes if you so desire.

In general, for comfort's sake, it's best to have the woman of the couple approach the third. A man approaching a woman for sex,

46

whether at a bar or online, will not receive a positive response. It often comes across as creepy.

Approaching women together is usually off-putting. Say that you have a couple's OkCupid profile and you both use it to send messages. Your potential third won't know who she's writing to or who will read her message at any given time. It doesn't build comfort or trust.

In person, being accosted by a couple is even more overwhelming for a single woman than being hit on by a guy is. Your potential third may even feel unsafe.

Having the woman do the talking is the best method. A woman can come across as more low-key, befriend the third, and bond with her in a girly way.

Note, however, that you should be honest about your status and your intentions. Don't let a girl in a bar assume that you're single and then when she's all heated up and ready to come home with you, spring the fact on her that you're in a couple.

Keep your third comfortable as you go through the steps of seducing her. Communication should be open and honest among all three parties. Check in with her every so often to make sure that she's feeling good about what's happening and wants to continue.

Maintaining comfort keeps everyone happy.

Respect
You should always keep in thought how your potential third is thinking and feeling, and respect these thoughts and feelings.

Your third is a person. This should go without saying, but for many couples, it doesn't. A Clueless Couple thinks only of themselves, never considering the needs or wants of their third.

For example, some couples will plan out boundaries, such as "The man in the couple can't kiss the third," or "The third must leave immediately after sex." In many cases with NSA sex, the couple wants the third to disappear after the polyamorous simply. The problem with this thinking is that the third has not been consulted.

What if the third is not willing to have sex without kissing? What if for the third, half the fun in sex is cuddling afterward? Or what if the third isn't aware that the polyamorous is a one-time occasion?

Another example is when both members of a couple get off in a polyamorous and then expect the third to leave. If her needs aren't taken care of, the third will wonder why they don't care that she hasn't had an orgasm. She certainly won't want to come back and play with that couple again.

It is necessary to remember that a third is not a living sex toy that can be brought into the bedroom to spice things up, then cast away as needed. Nobody wants to be treated like a used Kleenex, something to be thrown away when no longer required.

Your third's physical and emotional needs and desires must be taken into consideration. This can be hard to remember when she's just an idea and you haven't even found her yet. But considering how many options a third has for who she chooses to sleep with, her satisfaction should be of the utmost concern.

That isn't to say that couples can't have boundaries or know what they want. Just bear in mind that your third is a person, with wants and needs. A couple needs to be flexible on what they are willing to do and needs to communicate with the third about what all three people are looking for.

One polyamorous participant explained her feelings in a Reddit post. "It's not that people shouldn't set the boundaries they need to; of course they should. But please treat all your sex partners, including women who join you for a polyamorous, as human beings and equal participants, not just a stand-in occupying the hole in your fantasy."

Standing Out
Whichever method of approaching a woman you choose, you will want to make yourselves stand out from other couples. You're one in a crowd, and you need to differentiate yourselves somehow so that a potential third will notice you.

The main thing is to not just talk about what you want. Talk about what you have to offer.

An example of a Clueless Couple's post on, say, Craigslist could be as follows. "Hey, we're looking for a fun girl to join us in the bedroom! She must be 20 – 25, white or possibly Asian, and skinny. We both like big boobs. And please be SHAVED, or we won't even think about it!"

Do you see the problem here? The couple has only told the world what they want. Even if a big-boobed, skinny, shaved white woman in their age range reads the message, there's nothing to make her want to contact them because she has no idea what's good about them. She doesn't even know what they look like!

In the meantime, the Clueless Couple has alienated every woman who doesn't meet their strict criteria. Again, you're one of many options a potential third can choose from. I don't want to say you should lower your expectations, but you'll probably have to be flexible.

An example of a better Craigslist post: "Hey, we're a young professional couple living downtown. We're hoping to find someone to join us in the bedroom, either one time or for an ongoing thing. He is 25, white, tall, fit, and loves giving multiple orgasms. She is 24, mixed, slim, shaved, and inexperienced with women but eager to try. Drop us a line if you're curious for some casual fun with a sexy couple!"

This couple has described what they have to offer a woman. She can decide if she's into their physical characteristics and their sex style or kinks. It's even better if you attach a picture so she can see just how sexy you are.

Who To Approach
If you're like most couples, you want a bisexual woman. Of course, she also has to be hot. The Clueless Couple's requirements stop here. They will message or go up to every woman who might be bisexual that they find attractive. However, there are some other factors to consider.

Ashley Madison's blog recommends that you make "a mental polyamorous partner checklist" to start with. Decide what traits are mandatory and which are desirable. According to an Ashley

Madison members' poll, these are the most common traits people want in a polyamorous partner:

- "Sexy (and who doesn't want some sexy in their lives?)

- Sexually open (We don't need your life story, but you should be open to new experiences)

- Not jealous (and laid back for that perfect polyamorous experience)

- Communicative (communication is key in a polyamorous)

- Shameless (shyness has no place in a polyamorous)"

In general, you should be reasonably sure the woman you approach is interested in casual sex. If a girl online is looking for platonic friends or even for dates, even if she's hot and bisexual, you will be wasting your time and irritating her by writing to her.

For some people, kink and fetishes may be an important consideration. If you and your partner are extremely into BDSM and have your hearts set on a BDSM polyamorous, finding a vanilla girl might not be satisfying for you.

Then again, sometimes you can find a willing woman who doesn't fit your requirements.

The woman doesn't necessarily need to identify as bisexual. She might be bi-curious or even a flexible lesbian, but if you're looking for a true MFF polyamorous, she has to be into both of you.

For example, in a recent Savage Love sex column, a woman wrote in that she was planning to join a couple for a polyamorous. She was straight and was listed as such on her OkCupid profile and had no interest in giving oral sex to a woman, but was open to receiving it. Depending on your wants and needs, a "straight" woman like this might be just fine for your tastes.

It also might not be necessary for the woman to be single. You could approach a woman in an open relationship or a swinger couple if she meets your other criteria. Women in these situations may or may not be able to play alone without infringing on the rules of their relationship. It's worth asking!

But if you ever come across a woman online who says she isn't interested in men or polyamorous, though, just leave her alone. She could be a lesbian, not into casual sex, or simply irritated by Clueless Couples treating her like a piece of meat. In any case, writing to her is unlikely to get you anywhere.

You might consider finding a girl who's in a relationship for a foursome. These can be as hot or hotter than polyamorous. There's less chance of jealousy or hard feelings because all four people are already attached.

You can also do a girl swap with another couple. The girl from Couple A goes and has a polyamorous with Couple B. Then the girl from Couple B comes and has a polyamorous with Couple A. It's twice the lesbian fun for the girls, and both guys get to live out their fantasies. Of course, if you have any boundaries, like that the guy can just watch, these must be laid out in advance.

With the large pool of couples seeking polyamorous, it will be easier to find a couple that's had the same idea as you. You can look for a couple in almost all the same ways you can look for a single woman.

Chapter 8. Understanding The Polyamorous World

It's clear from the above explanation that a lack of understanding of - and interest in - a woman's world is what keeps men from connecting with these women.

And, to connect with them, a man will have to spend some time learning about what makes her tick, how she views the world as well as the men that she interacts with.

In other terms, if you require getting her to sleep with you and other women at the same time, you have to show her that you care, at least a little bit, about who she is as a person and what it means to her to be bisexual.

When I say 'care,' I mean that you care and learn to appreciate her situation... not that you just pretend to care. This is not about 'tricking' her into having a polyamorous with you. (If you want to enjoy the rest of your life, I would suggest that you not piss a woman off. ;-)

How Bisexual Women View Most Guys

So... since most guys have no clue how to approach or talk to a bisexual woman, that is what women usually experience when dealing with most guys.

Most women assume before a guy even opens his mouth, which he is clueless about what it means for a woman to be bisexual. That he has no understanding, nor appreciation, for her unique and sometimes difficult life and social position. And, the handful of guys who do show an understanding of her and her life are absolute "catches" in her eyes.

In other words, not only will your chances of success with her increase dramatically by being that unique guy, but she will work on seeking you out because she knows how rare it is for her to find such a guy. When you take the time to 'get' what I will share in this manual, you will become one of those rare guys. And, you will be amazed at how women will start noticing that rare quality about you, even before you talk to them.

Women Want This Experience

The craziest part about this whole scenario is that women want to explore being with another woman. They won't find such a guy that will help them with this task. They want to experience what this type of guy can share with her. I may even go as far as to say that some women cry out for it because it's so unusual for them to find such a guy. It's no secret that, as a species, women are more open-minded - and often more evolved - than most men. That's just the fact that men need to accept and embrace. Women are more in touch with themselves, their feelings, and everything around them. They're more intuitive and more open to new experiences and adventures. Most women that I've met have thought about being with another woman at least once. Most women have fantasized about it at least once. And many women, especially the more educated and modern ones, have experimented being with another woman, at least once.

So, all of a sudden, you recognize that a lot more women are bisexual, or at least bi-curious on some level, than you could have ever imagined! Oh, they will never admit to it, especially not to most men. In fact, many will seem offended and even appalled when asked if they are bisexual or at least bi-curious. (We'll discuss why this is so, soon.) But, that's okay. We're not concerned with that at all. I'll share some techniques and concepts you can use to take care of all that.

The most important thing in all of this is for you to realize that at least half the women you'll be meeting out there are either bisexual or bi-curious – whether they will want to admit to it or not. And, as our society evolves and opens up more, the numbers will only increase). That one realization alone will be responsible for the majority of your success in this endeavor.

Even if the woman you meet is not necessarily bi-curious, i.e. she's not interested in finding a woman to experiment with, you may still be able to interest her in a polyamorous… IF you structure the opportunity for her in the right way.

As mentioned earlier, women are open-minded, to begin with. Also, many of them are simply bored in the bedroom (since most guys aren't all that great in bed).

And, even if they aren't necessarily bored, they crave the experience of doing something different. Something that will help them learn more about themselves.

It's a very natural thing for women to want to explore and learn more about themselves, their thoughts, feelings, bodies, and their lives. It's just how they are created. And they are also very curious by nature.

So, even if a woman may not be interested in seeking out a bisexual experience, if it's there and if she feels comfortable and safe around the guy she's with, she will very likely go for it when the opportunity is presented to her. (This is true. It's not theory; it has been tried and tested many, many times). She will be open to the idea if presented in the right context – by the right man! If you're the kind of man who has already shown her that she can learn from you, that she can expand her capacity for pleasure and experience through you, and if she feels comfortable and safe around you, she will have no problem trying a polyamorous with you. (You will learn how to do all of the above). This is very powerful knowledge to have, and most men will never believe, let alone learn, about this.

The fact remains that many women will enter the situation being straight and find themselves kissing another woman before the night is over. It appears more often than you can imagine. They are comfortable trying this experience with the right man… A man who "gives them permission" and makes them feel good about it. That's what most women want… They want to be given permission to do it and feel good about wanting to do it even before they try it. This is very important to know, and you'll learn how to go about doing this.

Why They Don't Want To Admit To It
So, if so many women are eager to explore with another woman, why are they so secretive about this part of their lives? And why do some of them even deny it or get angry if someone implies that they may be bisexual, or bi-curious?

There are many reasons for this, but here's one of the biggest ones...

We live in society, at least in the USA, where more than half the country still labels homosexuality - and by implication, bisexuality - as 'wrong.' Many of these people are even taught by their religious leaders that such a lifestyle is a 'sin.'

Some women struggle with this on a daily basis because they've been led to believe that something is wrong with them. That they are not normal.

It's sad.

Consequently, we have a society where this lifestyle is either led in complete secrecy or this part of many women is deeply repressed, sometimes even from their consciousness.

OR...you see the other extreme where people are holding picket signs and fighting for their right to live this way openly - and be treated equally and fairly.

It is a crazy world out there.

When you start learning these things, you realize it's no surprise that most women keep this part of their lives hidden from everyone, especially from most men. They simply assume, and rightly so, that most men (and most of society) just aren't ready to handle this part of a woman's reality. Add to that the previously-discussed fact that most men view bisexuality in a woman only as a means to get their rocks off, it all starts making even more sense.

Many women won't even admit to their longtime boyfriends or husbands that they've had this experience before (or that they have entertained the thought,) simply because they know that they will get pressured into trying it again, for all the wrong reasons.

Or worse... They'll make the guy feel upset or insecure about the whole thing. (Yes, some guys can be such primitive babies, especially when it comes to the subject of sex. They pretend to be macho and strong on the outside, yet on a deeper level, they just can't handle the reality of his woman being attracted to someone else – even if that someone else is another woman.)

It's no wonder most women will never talk to most guys about this stuff. That's all the more reason for you to be a different kind of guy.

Be the Man That She Is Searching For

By now, you have a pretty good idea of what most guys are like and why they don't get anywhere with women, in this situation.

You also have a pretty good idea of the kind of man that women are looking for.

Armed with the above knowledge, you are giant steps ahead of most men already.

Having an understanding of - and appreciation for - what she's about is very important. There's no better way to connect with her on a deep level than this, especially since most guys have no clue about any of this.

It will set you apart from the rest of the guys, making you look like the 'ultimate prize' in her eyes.

And, of course, you have to be the kind of guy who has already shown her that she can learn from you, that she can expand her capacity for pleasure and experience through you, and the kind of guy she feels comfortable and safe around.

Okay…

So, you already know what kind of guy she's looking for. But, how do you present yourself so that she will see you as one of those rare guys?

Be the Confident Leader

For any of this to work, you have to take on the leading position, from the very first time you talk to her about this, and all the way to the bedroom.

And, you have to be confident and comfortable with this leading role.

Women will only follow a man who they feel can give them new experiences, someone who is worthy of leading them through this journey.

(But never force or pressure a woman into it! If you do, it will come back to bite you either legally or in some other worse way.

Also, don't ever use alcohol or drugs to "get them ready." They have to be sober and consenting. That's always the best policy, in my opinion.)

Act As If...
I'll show you exactly what to say and do to project this leading quality.

However, if this is your very first time taking on this role, you'll simply have to act as if you're comfortable with the leading role. Go in with the belief that you're helping both her and yourself to expand your level of pleasure and experience. As long as you see it as a benefit for both of you (which it is,), it's all good.

Don't over-sell your stance or the opportunity you're about to present to her. Over-selling an idea can give the impression that you are desperate or unsure.

Your attitude should be that being with bisexual (or bi-curious) women and enjoying polyamorous is normal for you. And, while you enjoy this lifestyle, it's not a big deal for you. (Of course, this is the exact opposite of how most other men are.)

You'll find me advising to "act as if" a lot. The reason is simple: it works!

You'll find this same advice in almost every success or personal development book going back hundreds of years. So, it's not some wacky theory I've cooked up.

I've seen people's lives being transformed simply by starting their journey with the advice to "act as if" they already had what they wanted… Or that they already were who they wanted to be.

If you want to be successful, act as if you already are. And, you'll find yourself doing, saying, wearing, walking and emulating everything else like someone who is already successful.

That shift in your mind, body, and spirit will be felt by everything and everyone around you. And, they will respond accordingly.

Warning: This is not just about outer appearance. It's not just about changing your clothes and hair style. It goes much deeper than that. It's about embodying the personality of someone who is already successful. It's about becoming that person, even for a small portion of your day.

In this case, you want to embody the essence of a man whose daily reality is talking to women and easily convincing them to have polyamorous with him.

He is confident in this role because he knows that it works. And, he is relaxed and in control because he has no reason to doubt the results.

As absurd as it may sound to some people, you will start getting equally powerful results simply by embodying the role of this kind of man. (Obviously, you will need some practice with taking on this role, but that's true of anything new that you're doing in life.)

Once you have adopted the mindset and attitude, it's time to work on what you're going to say to her. (Words are nothing without the mindset and attitude to back it up.)

Make Her Feel Good About All of It
This section is where you'll learn how to impress the heck out of her, make her feel good about herself and her lifestyle (or curious thoughts,) and you'll also get her to start seeing you like the guy she would want to explore and share her bisexual side with.

You'll tell her things about bisexuality that most bisexual women don't even know! So, you can see why you'll be able to impress and educate her like no other man ever has.

Before we get into all that 'deep level' stuff, let's quickly cover something else first…

As discussed earlier, the mindset to adopt, when approaching women about this subject, is to assume that most women are already bisexual or at least bi-curious. And, also that this subject is completely 'normal and acceptable' to talk about.

By adopting this mindset, you're also projecting the sense that bisexuality in women is 'not a big deal'... That it's a normal and acceptable phenomenon – as far as you are concerned.

This mindset, combined with the other strategies we're about to discuss, will get her to start seeing you as a different guy – the kind of guy that she could open up to, about this part of her life, and know that she won't be judged or ridiculed. Maybe even the kind of guy that she could share this part of her life with.

She'll see that you're not just another guy who wants to check something off his fantasy list (a polyamorous,) someone who has no idea nor cares to find out what all this means to a woman.

Along with adopting this mindset, you also need to share some positive qualities and knowledge about bisexuality, to further comfort and validate her thoughts and feelings. While you do that, you will also create intrigue, interest, and even attraction in her mind – for you.

Let's get to the cool stuff...

You can start by telling her that bisexuality in women is a very natural, beautiful, and even a healthy phenomenon. (Some of the women may look at you with a little skepticism at this point. That's normal. And don't worry, you can back up the statements you made above.)

You can then talk about why bisexual (and bi-curious) women are different from 'ordinary' women. That they may even be somewhat superior and more evolved in some ways.

"Because bisexual women are more open and free...not just with their sexuality, but with everything in life. With every area of life. Both physically as well as mentally. Oh, and also emotionally, of course.

59

Because you see, this goes so much deeper than just sexuality. This sense of openness and freedom allows them to experience life uniquely and amazingly.

They're able to connect with people, life, and the entire universe on a level that most other women will never know. And, as a result, they're more intuitive, more aware, and more understanding of themselves and others... And of course, they're usually happier and fulfilled with their lives, as a result.

But, most importantly, they have come to realize something even more powerful... That it's all really about energy. And two Yin (female) energies nourish, nurture and strengthen each other...mentally, physically, and spiritually. It's just a natural way in which the entire universe functions (since everything is simply made up of energy).

Okay... if you're a typical guy reading this, you'll think that the above paragraphs are nothing special, that it probably won't make any difference to the woman.

If you're a woman (or a man who's more evolved than most) reading the above paragraphs, you're probably saying "WOW... those are some deep and touching revelations.

That's how women will hear it when you say the above to them. And that's why it resonates with them so well. That's why it works.

You can also tell her that...

"... this society that we live in today, the Western culture, is in many ways very young, and a bit backward, primitive and slow. However, the older and wiser cultures around the world, especially the ancient Asian cultures, where many of the martial arts, yoga, and tantra originated from (practices that we have only recently started to embrace again)... Cultures where people were more in touch with their true selves and connected with everything and everyone around them on a deeper and more meaningful level...

... In these cultures, two women caring, nurturing and comforting each other was a very special and beautiful thing. In fact, a young girl's first lover would usually be another, more experienced woman who would teach her about her body, and how to enjoy all the amazing pleasures (of mind, body, and spirit) as fully and completely as one ever could...More so than most of the women of today can ever experience.

Obviously, this wasn't just about a sexual or physical thing. It went so much deeper and touched the true essence of a woman. It was about nurturing and healing. It awakened her and made her blossom to her fullest. Unlike today's society where women are taught to repress their sexuality, and as a result, all other parts of herself.

And the women of today, who have boldly decided to get back in touch with what has been repressed for so long...These women who gain that sense of openness and freedom find the kind of satisfaction and fulfillment from all areas of life, including a deep and meaningful sexual healing, that other woman have no idea of.

You can even talk about how in today's world, women tend to be very jealous and competitive with each other...almost as much as, or worse than, some men. It's because they have suppressed, and in some cases lost, that part of her that can bring her the most fulfillment and healing in life.

And... when you see two or more women care for and nurture each other, even if it's in a non-sexual way, you find that they regain their real power and inner strength. And nothing, absolutely nothing can stand in the way of their happiness and inner growth.

All of the above stories and learnings that you will share with her have a central theme...That bisexuality is a natural, beautiful and healthy thing that should be embraced and enjoyed.

You're also making her feel good about the thoughts and feelings she's having or has had in the past. And you're giving her permission to entertain those thoughts, that part of herself that she keeps hidden from others, or locked away deep down inside. You're making her feel good about herself. And, that is a very powerful thing to do.

Finally, she's met someone (a guy no less) who truly understands this part of her, and seems to be even more knowledgeable about it than she is. That, again, is very powerful.

Important: While you're explaining all of the above to her, speak very naturally, in a relaxed yet confident manner. Don't try to be overly-convincing or persuasive. Just explain to her that these are the facts, this is how it is, and it's too bad that so many people feel like they have to suppress their true feelings (and power) because they don't know the truth...Or because society says so.

What I have just revealed to you in the above section is extremely powerful stuff. As you start to use it, you'll begin to see what I mean.

Let Her Give Back

Another way to approach this issue...Especially if you're already in a serious relationship or marriage, and are interested in exploring a polyamorous... Is to simply make her exquisitely happy first – both in and out of bed. When you can make a woman feel completely satisfied and fulfilled, at least in the bedroom, she will want to give back and make you just as happy. She may even ask you, "Honey, what can I do for you?"

In the above cases, it won't be so much about her being bisexual or even bi-curious. She will simply see the experience as giving you more pleasure. And, in the process, she too will get to try something new... And get to explore, and learn more, about herself.

(Most men never get to experience this...because most men don't have the skill - nor the depth of understanding - to take a woman to such heights of pleasure and fulfillment.)

Warning: If you are in an existing relationship or marriage, be very careful about going down this path. And, be sure that the woman is not feeling pressured or made to feel guilty about doing this for you, in any way.

And, even if she is fully consenting, there is still a possibility that your relationship may change in some way, after experiencing a polyamorous – especially if there are other pre-existing unresolved issues in the relationship.

If your association is not on solid footing (or even if it is,), you have to decide whether going the polyamorous route is worth the risk. It is completely your decision and responsibility.

Also... If you do choose to do it, make sure that the 3rd person (that is, the other woman) is a stranger, not a close friend or acquaintance. Involving a friend in something so intimate and unknown can, once again, create unforeseen problems for all of you, down the road.

Chapter 9. Managing Multiple Women

A few more tips on managing multiple women, i.e. the 'circle dynamics'...

Whenever there is more than one woman in a group setting, each woman will multiply the relationship dynamics. It's very likely that jealousy and other issues will come up from time to time.

As the lead, you will have to put a stop to this the moment it surfaces. You will need to be firm and clarify what is and is not 'acceptable behavior.'

Bitching and moaning are simply not allowed in the circle. The goal is to have fun, enjoy each other's company – as friends and lovers.

Talk it out, get to the bottom of the problem, and get everyone on the same page – and happy. The same will apply to your primary, and her issues, even if she is your #1.

If you do not handle this right away, one unbalanced woman will put the entire circle off balance, and it will affect everyone until the circle finally collapses.

You will have to be the calm, relaxed leader that keeps the circle in line and keep everyone happy.

If you're confident and comfortable with what you can teach them and share with them, to help them learn more about themselves and grow, they will follow you, and they will respect the rules you've set.

You will also need to be cautious in how you treat each one of the women, and that you don't play favorites.

If you buy them gifts, be sure that everyone gets the same thing...The same size, the same color, the same amount, etc.

This also applies to intangible gifts.

If you don't do this, they will attach a value to whatever is different from their gifts and will start feeling unnecessarily negative about the situation. This will, of course, develop into something more serious over time and affect the circle dynamics.

Be aware of this and do your part in maintaining the balance of the circle.

The more they learn to work with each other and trust each other, the more their relationship with each other will grow and strengthen. They will know that they won't be replaced (unless they mess up in a major way.) And that will encourage them to want to work together and make the circle a great place to be.

How to Find Bisexual and Bi-Curious Women

Towards the beginning of the manual, I mentioned that the main focus of this manual would be on making polyamorous happen with the women you were in an existing relationship with, were already sleeping with, or women that you were already in communication with (with the intent of starting some relationship.)

And, while I've stuck to that goal, for the most part, I would like to give you a little extra – a bonus, if you will – that will help you find and interact with new bisexual/bi-curious women if you choose to do so.

This section will also come in handy if the woman you're already with decides that she's not interested in exploring bisexuality, despite your best effort…And if the two of you decide to part ways.

Let's get to it…

What to Look For
You've already learned that bisexual women are more open and comfortable with who they are.

So, naturally, they're also more open and expressive in the way they present themselves to the rest of the world. They don't try to blend in with or conform to, the rest of society.

As such, they will usually be very trendy and fashionable. They will stand out more, wear interesting and unique jewelry and accessories, and they will often have attractive and expressive tattoos. (Tattoos on their lower back, just above the waistline, is also common among bisexual women.)

(Plus, let's not forget that they're trying to get the attention of other women as well – which is yet more reason for them to stand out and look uniquely attractive.)

Also, because they're more open than other women, they will often radiate a very strong sexual energy. Both men and women will be drawn to this energy.

The next time you see someone who appears very sexual, without being slutty, you'll know exactly what I am trying to describe above.

(And, of course, if the woman you're in a relationship with currently or are married to, seems to fit the above description/criterion, the chances of her being bisexual/bi-curious is increased dramatically.)

Approach
Finding bisexual women is the easy part! Seriously. It's the rest of the stuff that's almost impossible for most men: interacting with, and attracting, these women.

Of course, you won't have that problem because you have this manual, filled with all the tried-and-tested power strategies that most guys will never know about. When you find a woman who you think is bisexual or bi-curious, your initial approach will be driven by the same mindset and attitude as previously discussed. You'll be relaxed, confident, very comfortable and straightforward about your approach. You will assume that the woman is bisexual, or at least bi-curious. Therefore, you won't tip-toe around the subject. You'll project the attitude that bisexuality in women is a natural, normal, and appealing phenomenon. And as such, all your questions, comments, and the entire interaction with her will display that same attitude.

You will also use your new-found knowledge about these women (that you learned earlier in this manual) to show them that you understand bisexual women, and their world, on a very deep level. (This is what will get you "in" like nothing else). When you do that, you will become very attractive in the woman's eyes (as we've already discussed earlier).

Since you have just met these women for the very first time, at this point, you need to create an emotional connection with them and then move to creating states of arousal. You can then present them with the opportunity to explore and learn more about themselves (since you've already established that they can learn new things from you).

And, through all of the above, you can also imply that you have other choices besides them. However, you're offering them the opportunity because you feel they are smart and unique enough to go for it.

Chapter 10. Unicorns & Butterflies

Polyamorous bisexual women aren't typically interested in closed relationships, or any close relationship for that matter. Couples new to polyamory who want a closed triad will naively seek out their third partner in the poly community, trying to get a poly lady to stop being poly and have a monogamous-style relationship with them. The term Unicorn Hunter is a derogatory term used for these poor naive couples, who are seeking the mystical HBB (hot bi babe) that magically wants to join the existing relationship without fuss, and leave her poly ways behind her.

To find such a woman in the polyamorous community is rare, thus the term Unicorn. A woman being approached by a couple in this fashion can feel hostile and resentful towards the proposition, hence the derogatory nature of the term Unicorn Hunter. She has already chosen polyamory over monogamy for a reason. She may be interested in a poly-fidelitous relationship if she gets to know the couple, or forms a relationship with one person first, but it will likely be an open relationship until she decides otherwise on her own.

Because Unicorn Hunter and the concept of unicorns, in general, are meant as an insult and do not embrace the kind of woman who DOES want a closed relationship, it is necessary to coin new terms. Enter Butterflies and Butterfly Lovers!

Butterflies & Butterfly Lovers

A butterfly is a bisexual or bi-curious woman who is monogamous but wants to be able to show the full spectrum of her sexuality. She is mostly happy with monogamy, or she may even feel that if she were not bisexual, she would be perfectly happy being monogamous, but something is always missing. Butterflies typically fall within the range of 60-40 to 50-50 bisexual.

Why the term Butterfly? In mountain climbing, a butterfly knot is used to tie in the middle person when traveling three to a rope. The knot is strong and can take a load from any of the three directions, (no pun intended) independently or simultaneously. Also, women suited to closed Three relationships, like butterflies, can be delicate and elusive. They are not however mythical and impossible to find as the term unicorn implies. Thus Butterfly & the men who love them, the Butterfly Lovers, are more appropriate ways to describe those drawn to this lifestyle.

Why is there not a word for the couple? Well, the reason that Unicorn Hunters is not fitting is that every woman in a couple seeking a triad relationship is technically a Unicorn. It occurred to me then that they could not possibly be as rare as everyone has believed them to be. So, there is no name for the couple. It is only that a butterfly loving man has found one butterfly to love, and together they are looking for another.

Cosexual
Cosexual is a new label for a bisexual woman who knows her relationship preference is relationships. It isn't just an option for her; it is the preferred option. She isn't interested in dating a man and a woman in separate situations to get what she needs. She is happier and feels more whole engaging in relationships with both sexes at the same time.

The term sexual in this context is derived from its usage in plant sexuality studies. A sexual plant possesses both sex functions. Most cosexual people don't have both sex organs like cosexual plants do, but their brain chemistry allows them to function equally well with both men and women sexually. Cosexual is also derived from the word "coed," meaning a woman who attends a co-educational institution. A coeducational institution is one that educates both men and women together. In fact, a coed facility or event of any kind is open to both men and women at the same time, and so are cosexual women.

Polyamorous intrigue and satisfy a cosexual woman because she can be all of who she is within one system. She knows that polyamorous offers her the perfect mix of the benefits of a closed, monogamous-style relationship, with the opportunity to express all of who she is all at once.

She has usually spent time loving both men and women to some degree but has had trouble finding fulfillment in the trappings of the "one-at-a-time-only" paradigm of monogamy. She is monogamous and enjoys the exclusivity of it, but has become aware of her need and enjoyment of expressing both sides of her sexuality concurrently.

She wants to live her true sexual identity openly; if not for the whole world, at least in her bedroom. Traditional monogamy has no solution to resolve the bisexual/monogamous conundrum for her, and she refuses to conform to the world that erases who she is as a bisexual woman. For a sexual woman, polyamorous are her sanctuary.

Why Embrace a new Label?
Self-allowance is the key to true happiness in life. So if you are a square peg in a world of round holes, you will need to embrace your edges and build a new paradigm that fits you to find your bliss in life. Labels like cosexual, butterfly, and polyamorous serve to offer new ways to define ourselves more accurately in the world. Asking yourself how you should live your life might be the question, but the answer has nothing to do with figuring out what to do. It begins with figuring out who you are, what your preferences are, what brings you joy, and what turns you on the most. There is no one right way to do life, but there are right ways for you. Once you can accurately define who you are (find an appropriate label) all the instructions and how-to be's will unfold. What to do next won't ever be a question again. How amazing is that?

Polyamorous and the Spectrum
While anyone, no matter where they fall on the spectrum could form a very happy triad relationship, those that fall in the 60-40 to 50-50 range are most likely to find fulfillment from such an arrangement. The reason is that the center group are the ones that seem to have a harder time resolving their conflicting desires while practicing monogamy. Desires that are easily met in a polyamorous.

If you don't fall into that range on the spectrum and you're still interested in polyamorous don't fret. The only thing required to make any relationship work is the willingness to make it work. It is necessary to be clear with your couple about where you are on the spectrum. For example, you might not be into women enough to be interested in going down on your female partner, but you're good with her going down on you. The woman in your couple may be perfectly fine with that. She might not be. Just be willing, to be honest, and accept the honesty of all involved. If you find everyone isn't in agreement about what everyone wants, better to know right up front.

If they aren't for you or vice versa, there is a couple out there perfect for you exactly as you are. The relationship is about acknowledging and honoring the truth of who you are, not about compromising those truths. That doesn't mean you shouldn't be willing to try something you've never done before; it just means you don't have to do things you have a solid knowing you don't like or want. Whatever your desires, don't ever be afraid to be completely honest. Honesty is what polyamorous are all about!

Polyamorous Basics
The inner workings of a polyamorous can seem confusing to people at first. Not because they are particularly complicated, but because it's something most people have just never thought of before. As you learn more about how polyamorous function, you will find that the concepts are not new to you. They are just ways of interrelating that you already know, applied in the area of love and romance.

Most people have embraced the concept of polyamorous in general, meaning casual polyamorous sex. It's relatively common place these days and easy to wrap one's mind around. Once someone throws in the idea of an ongoing relationship between those three people, for some reason, all hell breaks loose in people's minds. To try and ease some of the crazy and to bridge the two ideas, the most simplistic explanation I have come up with is this: a polyamorous is like having a polyamorous every night, but with the same two people. You're getting all the fun and excitement of a polyamorous, as well as the depth and intimacy of a committed relationship. Who wouldn't want that? It sounds awesome because it is!

Anatomy of a Polyamorous
The triad is central, and three couples are formed. Though each couple has its identity, each is contained within the triad and is therefore not considered a wholly separate relationship. Each couple

intertwines and is interconnected with the others, thus functioning as one relationship unit also known as, "the polyamorous".

For the triad to function successfully, each person must nurture their connection with both partners, themselves, and the triad as a whole.

This may sound complicated, but everyone has families, groups of friends, and work groups that can be broken down into parts just like this.

Polyamorous Relationship Styles
Because of polyamorous function as one unit, as a couple does, there are also the same options of how to structure the relationship as there are for twosomes. These are…

Monogamous Styled or Closed- Exclusive, committed polyamorous. No sexual or emotional relationships outside of the triad without consent of the other two partners.

Non-Monogamous Styled or Open- Open polyamorous operate just like any other kind of open relationship. Partners are committed and bonded to the unit but can date or sleep with other people outside of the polyamorous in accordance with the rules and agreements that they have established with each other.

How the relationship gets structured is negotiated and agreed upon between the three parties. Typically a couple wanting a woman to form a triad ultimately wants a closed polyamorous, though that is not always the case. It's incredibly important to know which kind of polyamorous you are interested in and communicate openly and honestly about that to your couple. In the Communication section, we will go into more detail about how to negotiate what you want from your polyamorous.

Types of Polyamorous
One of the major misconceptions about polyamorous is that they have to be serious and committed romantic relationships or nothing else. The truth is that there are many levels of relating. Yes, some involve marriage and children, the rest do not. Many women who are interested in a couple say no to a polyamorous arbitrarily, because they assume the couple is only looking for someone to settle down with. In reality, every couple has many possible positions to

be filled in their lives. If you are all attracted to each other, it is guaranteed that one of them is for you. However, just because you are all drawn to each other doesn't mean you are meant to be their future wife or even a serious girlfriend. Sometimes it's something else.

You also have a specific position in your life that they would be equally perfect for, you just have to find out what that is. Sometimes it's meant to be "be all, end all" relationship that will last a lifetime. Sometimes it's not. Whatever it is, it is something, and shouldn't be ignored or dismissed.

Take the perspective that your own life is a company, and you are the head of HR. You need different kinds of people in different kinds of departments doing different kinds of things to make it successful. The positions are endless, and new ones can be created, or some let go of based on changing needs. It is your job to be aware of the positions available and the requirements needed to fill those positions. It is then your responsibility to match the right people to the right positions in your company. Looking at life this way can benefit you in any relationship process, but especially in polyamorous.

Find a position below that most closely matches your current needs, desired commitment level and benefits wanted. Keep in mind that the secretary of a company will not receive CEO benefits and treatment, and vice versa. Similarly, the responsibilities of a CEO will be much different than a secretary's. Benefits will always match commitment level and level of responsibility to the relationship. If you want to get more, you will have to give more. If you know that you want to be a CEO one day, but aren't sure if this is the "company" you want to commit to, start in a different position and exercise your option to ask for a "promotion" at a later time.

This list is by no means exhaustive, but it will offer some general categories to get you started. Once you find one that is most like what you want, you can negotiate the details further with your couple. The open and closed styles still apply, no matter what position you want, though it becomes more important once sexual and romantic intimacy comes into play. Essentially, whether something is open or closed, in most cases, is like applying for a full-time position where you won't be working for anyone else or a part-time position where you will have other "jobs" as well.

Not every couple will have all of these positions available, but familiarizing yourself with them will help you understand better what you are wanting. You can then communicate early on what it is you are looking for. Making it clear right away what you're interested in allows you to know immediately if you and your couple are going to be compatible or not. Telling your couple what position you are "applying for" helps everyone. There isn't anyone wrong for anyone. There are just wrong "jobs" for certain people. When people get placed in positions they aren't suited or qualified for, no one wins. When you take the time to place people in your life in the exact places that are most appropriate for them, life is nothing short of amazing.

Each position listed below will have the type of position, the potential titles you may assume the position, the characteristics someone should have to be suited for it, examples of expected "duties," typical time commitment, usual length of position, and whether the sexual interaction is included or not.

Don't take this concept too seriously; it is intended to be silly and fun. However, that doesn't mean that it isn't very beneficial to look at things in this way. So do it, even if it feels strange at first. Not only will this help you define what you are looking for with your polyamorous, but it will also help you begin to define other positions you have available in your life.

All positions are eligible for "promotion" opportunities at any time. Promotion offers can be initiated by you or the couple. Keep in mind that positions like Girlfriend and Wife are usually not entry level positions. Typically you will have to maintain another role for a while first successfully. This is a great way for everyone to figure out if they like the "company" they are keeping.

Chapter 11. The Phases of Polyamorous

Because the couple is often already committed to one another, there can be a tendency to feel like you have to jump the gun and be ready for a commitment right away as well. Though the couple may ultimately want a committed situation, I promise they are not looking for anyone to want a committed relationship before any relating has happened. You have to start at the beginning, just like with any other relationship.

Building a relationship has phases, just like a "regular" relationship does. The first phase is dating, or getting to know each other. Then usually, the situation moves into a sexual arena, where partners can further get to know each other and decide if they are indeed compatible. Lastly, once a nice rhythm has been established, you can all discuss the kind of relationship you want to have. This is the phase where you can decide how serious you want the polyamorous to be, if you want it open or closed, what direction you want the relationship to go...etc.

The phases can happen in any order and can take some time or happen quickly. However, to form a solid polyamorous, all phases must occur. This is true regardless of order or timing.

Phase 1: Getting to know each other aka "Dating."
In this phase, you spend time getting to know each other. You will spend time with the two of them together, and you may also spend time with one or both of them separately. It's perfectly fine at this point to spend significantly more time with just one of them. It can make the transition into the polyamorous much easier for everyone. However, do not neglect that for the polyamorous part of the polyamorous to work in the long run, you must establish an intimate relationship with both people individually. This can happen without having separate time with each person, but you do have to have a significant point of connection with each person other than your mutual attraction to the third.

In this phase, they shouldn't expect you to know if you want to be committed to them right away. Yes, they may know they want a long-term situation with a woman, but they don't know if they want that to be you until they get to know you. The dating process should be treated as though everyone was single and meeting for the first time, in a way.

So in this phase, just do stuff you like together. Go to dinner. See some movies. Play some sports. Talk about yourselves. Figure out if your life philosophies are a good match. If you continue to enjoy each other's company and the chemistry is good, move on to the next phase.

Phase 2: Getting Sexual

Once it's been established that everyone likes each other, it's time to get sexual. If you've never had a polyamorous before, you might be a little nervous, and it may keep you from smoothly transitioning into this phase. That's completely understandable. Just talk with your couple about how you're feeling. If you don't open up about it, you may unknowingly prevent the natural flow of energy towards sexual activity altogether, which can lead to a lot of needless frustration.

Sometimes this phase happens first, and that's completely fine. If it does happen first, then do Phase 1 along with it. Even if the sex is phenomenal, you will still want to make sure you all like each other before continuing to phase 3. Again, even if sex is happening, that doesn't automatically mean you are all now in a committed relationship. That will be established in Phase 3.

Phase 3: Defining the Relationship

Once it's been established that everyone likes each other and enjoys being sexual with one another, then you can discuss where the relationship is going. At this point, you have all spent a significant amount of time together, and have had a chance to get an idea of what you would like out of the relationship. This is the point where the nature of the polyamorous gets defined and negotiated. The Communication section of this handbook goes into further detail about how to negotiate the details of the polyamorous.

If you're reading this, you probably already are or at least have been considering dating a couple for some time. If you haven't yet begun dating couples, here is a typical example of how the dating process goes.

Step One: Attraction
You meet a man or a woman you find incredibly attractive. (Perhaps you meet the couple together, but more often than not, you will meet one of them first.) You strike up a conversation, and you find out that they are involved with someone, but that they want a polyamorous. After you talk some more, you decide that you are intrigued by this idea, and you'd like to meet their partner and get to know them. Phone numbers are exchanged, and communication begins as any other potential dating scenario would. If you did meet them both at the same time, you will still usually gravitate more towards one person and will begin communicating with that individual at this stage. This initial imbalanced attraction is quite normal. Just go with it. You will soon find that if you are attracted to one person, it's quite easy to be attracted to their compatible partner.

Step Two: Schedule a Date
If you met the two separately, for a while, you would likely have a closer relationship with the person you met first. Again, this is completely normal. You will likely communicate with that person and schedule a date or a meet up where you can meet their partner in person if you haven't already. A great way to get the ball rolling is to FaceTime when they're both together or start a group text thread so you can ease into communicating with the new person. Whichever one you began communicating with first, it's their responsibility to facilitate the initial relationship with you and their partner. At least until you find some common ground with which to develop a real connection with the new person. This may seem a bit strange to you or a newbie couple, but it's vitally important to the success of the polyamorous if the relationship with the other person is allowed to develop as naturally as the first one did.

Polyamorous is a product of three couples that happen to get along well together. It's important that each of those relationships has a natural and pleasant flow to it. You are not expected to navigate that on your own with someone you've never met before, especially if you aren't comfortable with it. If you are, go right ahead and communicate with their partner directly. They will love it! After all, you already have one great thing in common, attraction and appreciation for the other person.

If you don't immediately connect with the other person, don't force it. Take your time and find something that you both have in common you can talk about or do together. If you are really into one member of the couple, it is almost guaranteed that you will be able to see in their partner what they fell in love with too. Allow it to happen naturally. It's okay if at first, you vibe more with only one person. As long as you honestly intend on getting to know both people with the intention to date both of them, then it's okay to focus more on one person initially if it's easier for you.

Step Three: Date Night
The first date may be a little bit awkward at first, and that's perfectly normal. Just relax and be yourself. Remember that the couple is excited and nervous too.

There tends to be quite a bit of communication already in the established couple's relationship, so the other person will likely know whatever their partner knows about you. Embrace that. It's perfectly normal and actually, makes the first meeting and the rest of the polyamorous go much smoother when communication is open in that way. It's something you will get used to and grow to appreciate and count on as time goes by.

Whether you go to dinner or do something else, spend some time talking about your passions and goals in life. Find common interests and activities that you might all enjoy doing in the future. If you don't have everything in common, that's okay. It's really good if you have different things in common with each person. That will give you ideas about how you can use those things to develop a deeper relationship with each of them individually. You should have at least one thing in common with each of them, and some things that the three of you can enjoy together.

Step Four: Rinse and Repeat
If the first meeting goes well and you find you like and are attracted to both people, keep talking and going out on dates with them. There isn't anything special that has to happen. If you like spending time

with them, keep spending time with them. Remember that you don't have to know if you want a committed relationship just yet. Just enjoy the time getting to know each other and develop some emotional intimacy with each person.

Don't forget to spend at least a little time with them individually if you can. The three of you don't ALWAYS have to be together. Taking occasional one-on-one time is essential for developing your own unique "coupledom" with each person. You should feel like you want to spend time with each of them fairly equally, but it doesn't have to be for the same reasons, and in fact, it's great if you like them for different reasons. That's one of the things that's awesome about polyamorous, more people to experience the varieties of life with!

Polyamorous Dating Do's and Don't's
DO relax. Just because they are married or in an established relationship doesn't mean they expect you to meet their commitment level right off the bat. It's perfectly fine to test the waters and date for a while before you decide you want to be in a committed relationship with them. Treat the dating phase the same as you would with a single individual.

DO respect them as you would any other individual you were dating. Don't assume that because they have each other, they don't need the same common courtesies you would extend to someone who was single.

Don't expect to be the only person they are dating if you are not willing for them to be the only people you are dating. Exclusivity is a two-way street. Demanding loyalty before you commit is not cool.

DON'T ask advice about your new situation from people who aren't familiar with polyamorous relationships, especially before you engage deeply with your couple. Many people still don't understand and will try to talk you out of something potentially amazing because of their discomfort with the subject.

DO talk to your couple about anything and everything that concerns you about your interactions. Polyfidelitous couples tend to be incredibly good at communicating and prefer everything out in the open.

DO ask all of your questions. Polyfidelitous couples are typically more than happy to walk you through anything you don't understand. Since it's a relationship style that's new to a lot of people, they are used to having to explain things in detail.

DO be honest about your intentions, your reservations, and your wants and needs in the situation.

DO let go and have fun! Get out of your head and just enjoy these awesome people who are enjoying you too!

Chapter 12. Moving Things Forward

When you first invite them over to your place for the night, you can mention to each one that you have something special to share with them. This is just an added step that can make them feel special, cared for, whatever. The point is, it would make them feel good.

So, they already have an idea of what you may be up to. However, they don't want to feel slutty or cheap either. And, part of making them feel okay about the whole thing is to give the overall impression that it's all a spontaneous, natural and fun experience. Not something that has been cleverly planned and organized by you.

Yes, that means, you should not have the lights dimmed and Barry White playing on the stereo when they walk into your place.

Instead think of it as inviting two of your buddies over, to just chill and have fun.

Start off by playing a game or something…Charades, board games, etc. If you have something unique, like tarot cards or some new game (even a video game,), that's even better. (Obviously, stay away from games that are too much of 'blood and gore.')

Any game that gets a little into people's personalities, or something else that's intimate, is always great. There are many adult games out there as well, that can be intimate without being overly sexual. It's more a way of opening up and learning about each other.

Watching a comedy movie or show is also great. Humor is a great way to open people up and get them to relax.

You can even look online for those '20 Questions' type of games (or make up your own) that you can ask everyone, and each person has to take turns answering, and revealing something a bit personal and intimate about themselves.

And, of course, pay attention to the energy in the room! If it starts getting weird, back off a little. Take a break or switch to something lighter for a minute. (This piece is very important.)

Remember to keep it fun and interesting throughout the evening.

Also, by taking things slower than what they're expecting, you may also get them to want you to move forward a bit faster. And, that's always a good thing!

If the energy of the room, and of the women, is good, move on to something more intimate.

Massage is always great. If guys only knew what a good massage could do to relax and open up women, they would step over each other to take the next massage class immediately.

If there are 3 of you, two of you can pair up and give the other person a massage together. Then, you can switch.

At this point, you could also imply that you don't want to stay up 'too' late, which will again make them feel more comfortable in knowing that you're not just interested in getting them naked. They may even think that the massage is as far as they'll go for the night.

It's also important to note that if they are there with you, it's what they want to do. They have chosen to be there. (If they don't want to continue, they'll either tell you or telegraph it through their body language and energy.)

From here, you can progress to more sensual touching, and even kiss one of them.

Always kiss the primary first. Then kiss the other girl(s.) Keep in mind that you have already been sexual with each of these women individually. So, kissing won't be such a big deal, and at this point, it would feel like a natural progression of the evening.

(You could even get into something fun like body painting, etc. to keep things light, fun yet also moving forward. I can't tell you exactly which activity to do when. Each situation is different, and it would be arrogant of me to assume that I know exactly how your evening will go. As long as you keep it fun, light, and enjoyable, you'll do just fine.)

Continue to Lead

Maintain your confidence and leading role throughout the entire process...From the very first time you bring the subject up and all the way to the point when you're having sex with them.

Remember, women are very intuitive and can sense your energy. If you're unsure, uncomfortable or nervous about any of it, they will sense it, which will cause them to also feel unsure and hesitant about continuing.

They will start feeling that maybe you're not the guy who's worthy (or competent) of taking them through this experience.

So, you will need to maintain the leading role in the bedroom, especially if this is the very first time for at least one of the women in the group.

They will look to you to take charge and lead the experience.

So, continuing from the earlier section, you would start by kissing the primary first. Kiss the other girl(s) next.

And since you're in the leading role, you would then tell them to kiss each other on the lips. Then, have one of them move to something else (kissing on the neck, or whatever.) And tell the other one to do something as well (caress the other person's breasts, etc.)

Getting them started is important. After you get them going, they will continue on their own and please each other in ways that come naturally to them.

At that point, you can watch, join in, help out, etc.

Maintain the leading role but don't rush anything. Remember, that the main idea is for everyone to have fun and enjoy the experience as much as possible.

You can try blindfolding one of them

They will go along with it, as long as they feel that you are comfortable and secure in what you can teach them – about themselves, about new pleasures, etc.

It's important for guys to understand that women prefer their other four senses over vision/sight when it comes to experiencing pleasure.

Blindfold them, gently brush the tip of a fresh rose over their body, etc. Get all their other senses involved with different textures, smells, tastes, and so on.

The Day After
The day(s) or even hours after the main event, i.e. the polyamorous, can be interesting and you should have some idea of what to expect.

While all the women may have connected well and enjoyed each other during the actual event, things may change afterward.

Some women may want to get together with you and the other women again, others may decide to move on, and yet others may want to continue seeing you but not the other girl(s).

None of this has any deep, significant meaning. Take it for what it is.

The women that decide to stick around and continue enjoying future adventures with you and the other girl(s) are the ones you should focus on. Don't spend too much energy on those that decide to move on, and don't worry about trying to convince them to stay.

For you to enjoy future experiences, without too much drama, it's best to follow the above advice, and strategy…And only keep the women that connect well with everyone else in the group.

Important: Also, if you have a strong, balanced relationship with the primary, and she decides that the other girl(s) don't feel right to her, don't ignore or brush off her feelings. Take what she's feeling into consideration and make a decision that's best for everyone.

Also keep in mind that if you have a good, trusting relationship with the primary, she will willingly go out to find and attract other bisexual women for the two of you to try out.

Forming Your Own "Circle."
If you find that you enjoy the experience of being with more than one woman at the same time, not just on a physical level, but also on an emotional and spiritual level, you may want to consider forming your own "circle."

A circle is an arrangement where you're in a relationship with 2, and up to 5, women – with you being the only male.

Again, this is not about brushing your ego or acquiring 'bragging rights' so you can impress your friends or others around you.

This is serious. Real women, with real feelings and lives, are involved here.

So, if you decide to form a circle, you have to go all the way. You can't hide your lifestyle from others, at least not for long, if you want your 'circle' relationship to grow and evolve.

If you have to keep it a secret from your family, it's not a real circle, and will probably not last for too long.

Also…as mentioned earlier; you will need to have a primary, especially in a circle. The primary will be the woman whom you consider to be your #1 girl, the one you connect with the best.

Together, you and she will work on maintaining the circle (you being the lead, and her being the #1 girl.)

The relationship that you form with her is very important. She will need to feel secure, protected and safe in knowing that she's your main girl. That she won't be replaced. And the two of you will bring others into the circle and decide if they're compatible for a longer-term position in the circle.

Your primary, i.e. the #1 girl, will also take on the role of training the other women, the newer members of the circle, about the rules and etiquette of the group.

If a new member to your circle does not respect the rules and etiquette that you have set, it is your job as the leader to get her in line, or even let her go completely.

Never forget that you're the lead. Be firm about the rules no matter how hot the new member is. Don't favor her or put up with her just because you are excited about the polyamorous that you'll be having later.

If she's not a good fit for the circle, you'll need to fire her. Doing so will also build more trust and closeness between you and the primary. She will see that you're not just doing this for polyamorous sex. That you care about the relationship.

You got her into the circle by being a different kind of man. And, you'll have to maintain that position all the way through. (As I said earlier, this is serious. You have to be all the way in or all the way out. There's no 'on the fence' position in a circle.)

Chapter 13. Rules, Boundaries And Preferences

Once you've established the goals for the new relationship, you can begin to flesh out your rules, boundaries, and preferences. Rules are absolutes. Things that are NEVER okay like physical violence, cheating, stealing..etc. Boundaries are needs. They are the lines between what you are comfortable and not comfortable with.

Preferences change often based on mood and experiences. Boundaries usually take more time than preferences to change, but they will naturally evolve as the relationship evolves. Rules rarely if ever change. One example of a changing rule is opening up a previously closed relationship. Where before, engaging in relationships outside of the polyamorous would have been considered cheating, now it is part of the relationship agreement or vice versa.

Since preferences aren't required, they shouldn't cause more than a tolerable annoyance if not followed. With that being said, if they are rarely or never followed, it would be a good idea to have a chat with whoever is consistently choosing not to honor them. Small annoyances can build into full blown resentments over time. It's always best to address these as soon as it seems like it's becoming a pattern.

When boundaries are crossed...

Boundaries are things we need to feel safe, and secure in a relationship. Boundaries are trust zones. They are on the edges of us where we feel most vulnerable. When boundaries are crossed, it diminishes trust and requires a serious conversation to remedy. Too many crossed boundaries will lead a relationship to a place where the trust is irreparable. Any relationship, but especially a polyamorous that doesn't have trust is not a relationship at all.

Pushing boundaries is crucial to personal development and growth. However, when and how to push those boundaries is something that must be agreed upon by the person who has the boundary. It should never be pushed on purpose without their permission.

When rules are broken...

There are some broken rules that should and will be a one and done offense. Depending on the context, and the feelings of everyone involved, some rule breakers may deserve one more chance. Breaking the same rule again or breaking another more serious rule should be the end of the relationship immediately. Though it would be nice if 100% of polyamorous were as amazing and wonderful as they could be, they are made of humans, and no human is perfect after all. Though humans are imperfect, abuse of trust, physical, emotional, verbal, and sexual abuse is not a part of a healthy polyamorous and should never, ever be tolerated.

Remember, if something goes wrong in a polyamorous, it is not the relationship style that is the problem, but the specific people or situations involved that is the problem. Getting a bad meal at one restaurant does not mean that suddenly all restaurants have bad food. Same thing goes for polyamorous.

Addressing Concerns & Dealing With Conflict

The single most important thing about dealing with issues in polyamorous is to bring it to the table right away. Not that it isn't important to address issues in a monogamous relationship right away also, but it is extra crucial in any polyamorous situation. There is nothing like the way love magnifies and multiplies exponentially in polyamorous, but the same phenomenon that lets the love grow so fast can also accelerate the destructive power of negative emotions when left unattended.

If you are not sure that you are being reasonable or are too upset, consult with the one you do not have the conflict with. If you are having an issue with both people, talk to the one that is easiest for you to communicate with. Ideally, you should talk to the partner you conflict with directly. If you can, avoid putting the other partner in the middle. It's okay to consult with them if you are unsure, but once you are clear, you should talk to the partner in question yourself. Ultimately you have to remember that you have separate relationships with each person. As such, you may have different issues with each of them as well. Any issues should be resolved within the confines of the particular relationship the problems are coming from.

You can use the other partner as a mediator if you feel that would be beneficial, and if you feel they can offer a fairly non-biased viewpoint. They can act as a witness to remember things that were said during the discussion. This is a great benefit that isn't available in monogamous relationships. So many relationship problems come from misunderstandings, misinterpretations, or remembering what was said incorrectly. Having another set of ears is invaluable, and helps avoid future occurrences of the same issue.

So What about Jealousy?

Jealousy is by far the most common concern for newcomers to any poly lifestyle. This is true no matter what form of polyamory they are drawn to. There is a pervasive myth that polyamorous people don't experience jealousy. They do. It's just that most poly relationships are set up in a way that already encompasses the antidote to jealousy: good communication. What poly people know that you may not know yet is that jealousy is a symptom of something else. The ability to speak openly about one's fears, insecurities, and resentments is the key to resolving any resulting jealousy that may arise.

In polyamorous, jealousy is not as common as other poly relationships since the relationship is often closed. Meaning, jealousy happens more often in open relationships where members are allowed to have other partners outside of the primary unit. When jealousy does happen it is often an opportunity to ask oneself, "what am I wanting/needing?" Once that question is asked of oneself the next question is "How can I ask for it from my partner(s), or give it to myself?"

More often than not, the jealousy comes from needs and wants not being met that we expect someone else to meet for us. Usually, we can do a lot of those things for ourselves. When we can't, having the courage to talk about our jealousy and to ask for what we need is usually the perfect solution for any jealous feelings we may be having.

Jealousy is a wonderful tool for self-discovery because it spotlights our insecurities and where we feel that we are lacking. If we can look at first, anytime we feel jealous, we will learn to find ways to empower ourselves and find the wholeness inside of us that is always there. Whatever is left after that can be brought to the table and discussed honestly and openly with your partners. There you will begin to work together to find a solution that benefits everyone.

Clearing the Road
The real work of beautiful relationships is not the loving, but the clearing of anything standing in the way of loving. If you are willing to examine your fears and negative beliefs, you can find the treasure that was always waiting for you. In this case, the treasure is the ultimate bliss of complete self-expression you will find in polyamorous.

You may not initially like what I have to say about the topics in this chapter. That's perfectly normal. I am going to challenge some of your core identity programs. You might feel uncomfortable, you might feel resentful or angry at the truth I am asking you to witness in yourself. That's okay. No matter what your reaction, if you allow the realness to be, I promise you will be better, you will be truer, and you will be a more magnificent version of yourself.

Remember, you don't have to act on the truth you uncover. You don't even have to share it with anyone else if you don't want to. The truth is required, the action is optional. To be free, you must accept the truth of who you are, even if you do so silently, even if you never do anything with it, and even if you don't like what gets revealed. You might not. As the famous women's rights activist, Gloria Steinem once said, "The truth will set you free, but first it will piss you off." Getting a little pissed to get a whole lotta bliss though? Worth it if you ask me.

The most authentic version of you lies just beyond the words written on these next few pages. The most simple things that prevent women from saying yes to polyamorous are laid out here. You may have some of these in your mind already. You may discover some you didn't know you had. You may realize you're super ready, all you need is permission to proceed. Wherever you are in the process of saying yes to polyamorous, I give you permission to say YES to yourself. To say yes, right here, right now, and be the truest version of yourself. To know yourself, to honor yourself, and to own your deepest desires. You have full permission now, and forever more. And so it is…

Clearing The Heteronormative Program

Heteronormativity is the idea that what is normal and natural is to be heterosexual and monogamous. The truth about default programming is it is just that, the default. It was never meant to be the ONLY way. It is simply the most likely and probable way for a human to begin successfully operating most tasks in their current society. When you are born, you get default programming installed into your life by your family and the culture around you. This is so you can get up and living life. Once you begin to have your own experiences and discover yourself, you are supposed to customize your programming to encompass who you are fully.

It's a lot like the default programming that comes on a new computer. Everyone gets the same stuff, no matter what you will ultimately create with it. The standard issue programming is designed by imagining the most common needs people have. These default programs then offer the simplest, easiest to use solutions to meet those needs. A lot of people never require or want more than that.

However, if you discover that you have a passion for graphic design or photography for example, the basic paint application or photo editor is not going to get you where you want to go. Same goes for default life programming. If you find a basic default life isn't bringing you fulfillment, then you need to upload more sophisticated programs. Sometimes you have to write them yourself. There is absolutely nothing wrong with that.

Most people find some dissatisfaction with basic life programs. Instead of getting new ones, they just feel like there must be something wrong with them because they can't accomplish what they want with the options given to them in their default package. They fight against their own "abnormality" as though it is some fatal flaw that only they possess. They never begin to consider that they are just using the wrong program for what is truly right for them. Most people wanted to be normal and accepted so much so that they use the default programs given to them no matter how personally unhappy they become. The truth is, normal isn't real. Way more people are unhappy with standards of normal than are happy in it. Those people that are happy in it just happened to be born that way. Most couples who are actively seeking the polyamorous lifestyle, have already discarded their limiting programs and installed new ones that now allow them to be who they are true.

The biggest hurdle you will come up against in polyamorous, by far, is your default programming. No matter what ideas you may have to feel hesitant about the validity of polyamorous, they all come from the belief in heteronormativity. We all want to do things right. Heteronormativity says that to be right, you have to be straight and monogamous. Polyamorous completely oppose the foundation of that belief system. It is natural to have some concern about going against society's norms. The ego holds those beliefs in the deepest core of our psyches. It can sometimes feel incredibly dangerous to our self-identity to go against our instilled beliefs. The ego will try and come up with some reasons to hold on to the status quo to keep you "safe."

If the status quo doesn't allow for your happiness, however, you must allow the destruction of those limiting beliefs to be freed. In the future, society will completely embrace alternative relationship styles as part of the range of normal. For that to happen, everyone must be courageous enough to live the truth about their real preferences in love and life right now. The world won't change without anyone demanding that it does. Once the world can include alternative sexual identities and relationship styles in its definition of "rightness," choosing polyamorous will be as easy as choosing a hetero-monogamous one has been.

Polyamorous will sooner than later be just one of the many options in life that are acceptable choices for anyone. The truth is, it's already true right now, but your subconscious programming may want to disagree. Polyamorous is, in fact, a perfectly acceptable option for anyone who is drawn to it. It hurts no one and brings joy to so many. Unfortunately, the ego wants desperately to be "right" at all costs. Even if you know the default life isn't working for you, rightness is one of the ways the ego will try and keep you from stepping out of the box.

If you're too rebellious to do what's "right" by your belief system, the ego pulls out the big gun; GUILT. Therefore, if you do manage to step away from what you are "supposed" to be doing, the ego can use the guilt of being "wrong" to get you back in line with your beliefs. It's a self-preservation program that in most cases is quite beneficial. However, it can be a pretty nasty internal struggle when you decide that you want something, but it goes against some unconscious program or belief you are holding. At least the power lies within you. If you want to change, you can!

To stop the madness, you have to make what you are wanting right for yourself and believe in that rightness. The only means to do this is to be willing to know the truth of yourself. Then you have to choose to own the truth that you've uncovered. After that, you have to choose to live that truth, no matter what. You have to begin to make being happy and being true to yourself the new definition of "rightness" in your life. If you do that, what has been holding you back from many things will begin to dissolve. Make truth and bliss your new masters. They will without a doubt, lead you to a life of your dreams, regardless if that includes polyamorous or not. If you're reading this, it probably will include some form of polyamorous.

What about the Men?
You might be wondering now, what about the man in the situation? It's not a secret that most men can and do love multiple women at the same time. However, there are men who prefer to love more than one woman within the same relationship, openly and honestly. Not only that, but some men are for whatever reason, exclusively attracted to bisexual women. Coincidence? I think not. There are bisexual women in the world, and the answer for their ultimate self-expression is not monogamy. It just isn't. It's impossible to express the fact that you love two different kinds of people while only being allowed to love one at a time. The logical built-in solution to the monogamous bisexual conundrum is that there are other women like you, and men also made specifically to provide that lifestyle for you. He's not just happy to have more than one women because he's a man, he needs the relationship as much as the women do to achieve his full potential as a human being.

Common Concerns
I would be remiss if I didn't mention the specific concerns those new to this lifestyle may have. You may or may not have these yourself, but you have heard some from those around you who may not understand this lifestyle choice. The great news is there is

nothing anyone can think of that can't be resolved with a little bit of honest discussion. More than that, any concerns people have are usually pretty common and therefore easier to clear than you might think.

Below are the most likely "less-than-awesome" thoughts someone may have about polyamorous. If something is not on this list that you find yourself concerned about, just talk to your couple about it. There is always a solution to every seeming problem. You just have to be willing to find it...

"I'm not Bisexual."

Okay, good point. Lesbihonest here though. If you've gotten this far, the likelihood that there is already a couple you've found yourself attracted to is pretty high. You're curious. You have your gender preference, and suddenly, you like this person of said opposite gender you're not "supposed" to be attracted to.

If you're drawn to it, you owe it to yourself to explore it. I promise you that no one is drawn to things haphazardly. There is always something to explore. The truth is unless you have explored your sexuality extensively with all kinds of relationships, all kinds of people, and all sorts of configurations, you don't know for sure whether you'll like it or not.

I know many straight people, and I can tell you that there is never a time that they consider any romantic or sexual relationship with the same sex. Same goes for people I know that are all the way gay. So if you're curious or suspect an attraction, explore that. If you are considering this lifestyle even a little bit, something inside of you wants to be expressed, and that something is leading you to greater fulfillment of who you are. Honor it.

"It sounds too complicated..."

Breaking anything down into its micro steps would sound complicated. Take driving for example, if you had never driven a car before, explaining all of the steps that it takes to drive might seem like a lot to process. Once you start driving, however, you hardly even think about all of those steps. You just get in your car and drive. Polyamorous are the same. Breaking down all of the steps can seem laborious and complicated, but it's not. Once you just get in and drive it's really easy.

"I don't know if I have the energy/time to be with two people..."

If you're used to relationships where you were the one doing all the work to keep it going, then being with two people can sound overwhelming. The reality of a relationship is that it isn't any more work than being in a couple. All relationships take some work, but polyamorous have the added benefit of having one more person to share the workload with. This is especially true when sharing a household. Instead of being responsible for contributing 50%, you only have to contribute 33%.

"I'm so possessive/jealous. I don't know if I could share...etc"

First of all, if you are the single woman joining a couple for a polyamorous, you aren't the one sharing, they are. So take their lead. They're doing it for a good reason, probably because the benefits are worth it, because they are. Also, if the woman is willing to share her man with you and the man the woman, then there are probably some really good foundations of trust and certainty in their relationship. After all, certainty is the best cure for jealousy.

The other thing to keep in mind, because you are sharing someone doesn't mean you are getting less; you are getting double. If possessiveness is your thing, then why wouldn't you want two people who belong to you? Doesn't that sound divine?

"If we break up then I'll be alone, and you'll still have each other. That's not fair."

It may not seem fair, but their relationship has already passed through many obstacles and challenges that they have survived as a couple. Wanting everyone to break up, so you won't be the only one left alone is not reasonable. No matter what relationship you had had in the past when it ended you were alone. Just because the couple may still have each other, doesn't mean they would feel the loss of you any less. As individuals, they have each other to help them through the breakup. Just like you might have a best friend or confidant to support you through it. As a unit where being in a polyamorous is essential to who they are, they are left as alone as

95

you would be and have to readjust to life without you. It feels the same.

"I want this life, but I'll never be equal to his wife/girlfriend, so I want to start a system like this with a man of my own..."

This one makes my head spin. First of all, why if you have a perfectly great polyamorous in front of you would you want to go start over from the very beginning of the entire process? Remember, you are not a third wheel or some fancy accessory to the couple's closed relationship. You are a crucial component of a system that was designed for three people from the beginning. When you come together, you are beginning a brand new relationship with the three of you and with each. The fact that the two of them have an established relationship has no bearing on your value to the system. The status you have in the polyamorous is not time-based, but commitment level based. The benefits and place you receive within the polyamorous will reflect the place you CHOOSE to take. If you want it all, give it all.

As the person forming a polyamorous with an existing couple, you shouldn't expect to have the same privileges as the previously committed parties without first matching their commitment level. If you want wife benefits without wife responsibilities, that's not cool. Same goes with girlfriend benefits without honoring the actual commitment. Once you have established yourself as a permanent member of the relationship, then you will and should get all of the benefits of the pre-existing couple.

As far as wanting a "man of your own," the man in your polyamorous IS your man. If you commit to him, you ARE his woman too. Your relationship with him is no less important than his relationship with his other woman. She will and should insist on this as well.

If you are concerned because you want to be married and maybe have kids one day, that is still completely possible in a polyamorous. Many triads have children together as well as have weddings either as a polyamorous or as individual couples. Raising children with more parents is also one of the best things in the whole world. It takes a village you know. If you wonder what effect polyamorous have on children, reports show that adult children of poly families have had great experiences, felt a lot of extra love, and appreciated having extra adults to run to in times of need.

"It's not how I ever pictured myself or my life. It doesn't look like my ideal situation...etc"

We view the world from a fairly limited perspective, and we only know what we know. When we build an ideal picture of our love lives, we do it with the information that we have at the time. We do it with the options that are available to us at the time. These may not be all the possibilities that are available to us. The picture we hold in our minds isn't meant to be literal. It is meant to evoke the way we want to feel in life. Everything we choose to include in our ideal picture of what we want is a creation from our perspective of what our lives would look like if we felt the way we wanted to feel. The only reason we want anything in life is so that we will feel the way we want to feel when we have it.

We live in a world where monogamy and heterosexuality are the default program. Polyamorous are not something a lot of people grow-up knowing is even an option. The likelihood that as a little girl you dreamed of being with two people is pretty slim. That shouldn't stop you from wanting it now that you know about it. You didn't know that there were different kinds of foods or different places you could live than the ones you grew-up around. You wouldn't reject falling in love with another country simply because you never knew anything about it before. When you discover new things, you get to make new decisions about what you want in life. Something is amazing about that. You don't have to keep the picture of what you thought you wanted once you stumble across something different that feels as good or better. Drawing a new picture is okay. Changing your mind is okay.

If you are clear about how you want to feel in a relationship and life, that needs to be your only guide. You may feel frustrated or angry that what is making you feel so good isn't what you thought it would be. You may be mad at yourself for "settling" for something other than what you decided you wanted. You may still want to look for that ideal picture that fits more neatly into society's expectations of you, or your family's, or the ones you have for yourself. It may keep you from fully engaging in the polyamorous experience you have found yourself in. I strongly encourage you to allow yourself to be completely engulfed in what you are doing now. Do it all the way. Get all the way in it. It's the only way to know for sure if the polyamorous lifestyle is right for you. If you don't do it all the way because you're still secretly looking for what you thought you wanted, you would be doing your couple and yourself a great disservice.

"I don't know if I have the courage. I'm scared and don't know why...etc"

Don't be afraid of the fear; you just have to do it in spite of that fear. The danger is very real, but fear is not. If you are drawn to this lifestyle, there is something inside of you wanting to express itself. It is part of you. Denying who you truly are and what you want is the exact opposite way to finding happiness. You can't get there from there. The only way to be truly happy is to be who you are all the way, with no apologies. It can be really scary to be that vulnerable and expose hidden parts of yourself you think people won't accept. This is especially true if you're worried about what your family will think, what society will think, or what you will think of yourself for not getting that "ideal picture" of what you thought your life would look like.

The truth is, as long as you accept yourself and are confident and unwavering in it, the world will accept it too. Besides, anyone who would rather see you do life their way then for you to be happy only loves you conditionally. You should never be afraid to lose the conditional love that only serves the other person at the expense of your happiness, not ever.

"What would my family, friends, society think...etc"

If you find that living this lifestyle brings you joy and fulfillment why let other's opinions keep you from being happy? It is completely impossible to please everyone at once, and most who try are miserable for it. The truth is "normal" is an illusion. Hardly anyone fits into a standard mold of what society or families have decided are the rules everyone should live by. The only way to real happiness is making your way and sticking to it no matter what anyone else says. If someone loves and cares for you, they would want you to do what is best for you. They would require you to be happy no matter what that looks like.

With that being said, it is possible to live this lifestyle "in the closet" if you choose. In time, however, you are likely to find that the burden of hiding yourself is too heavy to bear. Clearing any shame and guilt, you may have about steering away from the cultural or familial norms is the key here. More often than not, any negative reaction you may come across is due to any potential uncertainties within yourself. Be strong, be proud, and own this part of you and others will accept it too, even if they don't like it. They may not completely understand it, or they may not understand it at all, but they will respect your solidarity and dedication to your joy. Who knows, it may even inspire them to live more fully expressed and uncover things that aren't so "normal" about themselves. Be a bold example, be a pioneer, show others they too can be free and blissful if only they stopped worrying about other's opinions and started following the pull of their hearts.

Dealing with the breakdown
These are by far the most common difficulties someone may have in their initial embarkment on the polyamorous journey. This list is by no means exhaustive. If you have these or other beliefs that you are working on, you may find yourself in some degree of an identity crisis. This is where the ego kind of freaks out about all the newness going on that challenges its preconceived notions about you and your life. You may feel a sense of loss or disappointment as you let go of the truths you once believed about yourself, and replace them with discoveries of who you are now. You may get frustrated or angry with yourself for not being more "normal" and want to cling to your old ways as a result.

You may feel like avoiding the situation to avoid those feelings. Do NOT do this. Running from your couple doesn't change the metamorphosis that is happening within you. You can run from them if you want to, but you cannot run from yourself. Woman up and deal with whatever surfaces head on. Being willing to face your shadow self will leave you feeling more clear, more whole, and more empowered than you ever thought possible.

Having uncomfortable feelings is quite common anytime you decide to change something you have always held true to yourself. It's not always easy to mine the diamonds within because they are often hidden by false beliefs and judgments of what you wish you were. Unfortunately, it doesn't matter who you want to be; it matters who you are. The process of clearing the way to embrace yourself as a bisexual woman who loves polyamorous can be challenging.

In any area of life, but especially in romance, you have to have the courage to accept the truth of what you like and what you are drawn to whether it's what you thought you wanted or not. It's the secret to the joy you have witnessed in others and perhaps has wondered how they got to it. After you sit with and acknowledge any uncomfortable truth, you will have to accept it and own it to be free of any negative emotions you feel about it. You can't unknow something you know. So once it is revealed to you, you may as well feel good about it. Unconditionally loving parts of yourself you wish were not true is the way to self-acceptance. Self-acceptance is the way to freedom. Freedom is the way to joy, peace, and bliss.

If you are struggling with something throughout your process, talk to your couple. One or both of them have most likely experienced everything that you might be going through and can offer you guidance. Speak openly about everything you're thinking and feeling. Yes, tell them even the thoughts you have, that you think you will be judged for. You probably know exactly which one or ones I'm talking about. You would be surprised, but it's often the smallest of thoughts that are actually in the way. Thoughts that can be easily cleared, simply by saying them out loud. So speak your mind, do it afraid if you have to, trust that you are on this path for a reason. Give it your all, and you will find rewards and treasures innumerable.

Conclusion

Obviously polyamory is not simple, nor easy. It requires honesty, trust, facing fears, healing past traumas and constant communication. It requires faith that it will all be okay, and the knowledge to walk away when use, abuse or dishonesty become obvious. It requires forethought and compassion, keeping promises, being reliable, following through, and keeping your word. It requires the ability to love someone new, without disregarding someone old. It requires more love and understanding when things get difficult instead of less. It requires patience and excessive communication.

The benefits are in not having to lie, cheat or steal and be yourself honestly. It affords a way for people to be as promiscuous or fidelitous as they are comfortable, without damaging others. It allows you to have more people in your life to love you, and for you to love, than just one person. It enables you to make your own rules about what you want in a relationship.